FROM
SNICKET
TO
Shakespeare

CONNECTING CONTEMPORARY
TALES TO THE CLASSICS

Lynne Farrell Stover

Fort Atkinson, Wisconsin
www.upstartbooks.com

To Dorothy Dell Taylor for suggesting the premise for this book during a Virginia Association for the Gifted conference.

Many thanks to the DIVAs (Destination Imagination® VIRGINIA) in my life for helping me appreciate how exciting and challenging it is to venture "outside the box."

And much appreciation to Roanoke College's Dr. Tim Reynolds and Dr. Leslie Murrill. Their annual Margaret Sue Copenhaver Institute has served me well as an educational energizer and creative catalyst.

Published by UpstartBooks
W5527 Highway 106
P.O. Box 800
Fort Atkinson, Wisconsin 53538-0800
1-800-448-4887

© Lynne Farrell Stover, 2006
Cover design: Debra Neu Sletten

CONTENTS

INTRODUCTION

Fantasy literature is more popular than ever. In fact, thanks to some outstanding writers, wonderful motion pictures, and the need for escapism in reading, there are students who refuse to read anything else. Parents are complaining, librarians are lamenting, and teachers are concerned.

It is the purpose of this book to help these students. While acknowledging the fact that fantasy literature is wonderful and important, we shouldn't let it be responsible for young readers missing out on some great books. If a student is a fan of fantasy that includes knights, wizards, castles, and jousting, let's put a copy of T. H. White's *The Once and Future King* in his hand. It just may become his new favorite book. Let's say that a very civic-minded young lady has read the 870-page *Harry Potter and the Order of the Phoenix* three times! It is our duty to guide her to other books that deal with social injustice and strong female characters. She will surely fall in love with *Number the Stars* by Lois Lowry and *Anne Frank: The Diary of a Young Girl.*

These are the connections—titles that are classics or award winners—that will take the student out of the realm of popular fantasy literature but keep him or her engaged in interesting and meaningful reading.

The extensions are 24 stand-alone lessons using fantasy literature as the "hook" to involve the students in skills lessons, creative writing, and innovative problem-solving activities.

How to Use This Book

This book contains 12 chapters, each focusing on the plot, setting, or characters in a specific piece of fantasy literature. Each chapter opens with a quote by a character or a passage by the author of the featured fantasy book. These were added to provide a connection between the selected piece of literature and the literary element highlighted; they are for the teacher's edification. The quotes may be shared with the students so that they may make the connection; however, they have not been incorporated within the lesson itself.

A synopsis of the featured book is included to help the teacher recall the basic content of the story. It should be noted that while the works selected include many contemporary best sellers, it is not necessary for the students to have read these books to successfully participate in the lessons. However, as many have been made into popular feature films, most students will be familiar with the plots, characters, and settings.

The titles recommended in the connection section of each chapter are suggestions for books that may be given to students who have read all of the Harry Potter or Lemony Snicket books and want another just like it. This is your chance to recommend a piece of classical literature or an acclaimed contemporary book to a student who has been reading fantasy literature exclusively. These lists are by no means all-inclusive.

There are two lessons included in each chapter. They are appropriate for students in upper elementary and middle school; however, they may be adapted for younger or older students. The lessons need not be taught in sequence, as each one stands alone. Most of the lessons can be taught in a 30- to 45-minute time frame.

The objectives listed in the lessons are general in nature and can easily be restated to apply to most curriculum content or mandated standards of learning. A National Standards Chart is included to help correlate local and state standards to the content taught in the lessons. **Note:** The standards in the chart have been paraphrased and should be used accordingly.

The materials listed are minimal. In most cases, an overhead projector for the transparencies; a water-soluble pen; the ability to mass-produce activity sheets; and some paper, pencils, and markers are all that is required.

Book Club Criteria

Many of the titles featured in this book would work well when used with a group of students as a selection for a book club or a reading group. Choosing a book that will be read by many people at the same time is an exciting experience and a big responsibility. In fact, you and your students are probably eagerly waiting for the next installment in a popular series right now! However, there are some matters that should be carefully considered before investing in a set of 20 or so books of the same title.

- Always read a book before using it with students—ALWAYS!

- Current copyright date is a consideration—it's no fun when half the group has already read the book.

- Consider your school's population when social issues are a part of a book's plot—when in doubt, find another book.

- Don't worry too much about the book's reading level—one way or the other, a willing reader will rise to the occasion and a strong reader won't be harmed.

- Main characters need to be compelling—the reader must CARE!

- Don't forget female and minority main characters—it won't hurt the boys to read about girls. (Kate DiCamillo's *Because of Winn-Dixie* has proven that.)

- Book length is no longer an issue unless you are working around a tight time schedule—we can thank J. K. Rowling for the fact that many students now think they have been cheated if a book has fewer than 400 pages.

- Do judge a book by its cover—given a choice, pick an attractive and detailed cover. This can set the tone for the visual learner's reading experience.

- The availability of an audiotape for the title selected is important—no student should be excluded from a Book Club due to visual impairment or a reading disability.

- Be prepared for "Another one just like this one please"—once you get the students "hooked" on a certain type of book, it is your responsibility to keep the supply coming!

NATIONAL STANDARDS CHART
STANDARDS OF THE ENGLISH LANGUAGE ARTS

National Council of Teacher of English/International Reading Association

Literary Concept	Lesson Skills and Activities	Standard
CHARACTER CREATION (CHARACTER)	**Lesson I:** Composite Character Creation - Creative use of literary characters **Lesson II:** Name that Character! - Create names for given character descriptions	**Lesson I** 1. Read wide range of texts (fiction) 4. Use written language to communicate effectively 11. Participate as a knowledgeable and creative group member **Lesson II** 3. Comprehend and interpret and evaluate text
ENGLAND: LONG AGO (SETTING)	**Lesson I:** Arthur's Journal - Writing for a specific purpose - Technical writing **Lesson II:** Diary, Journal, and Log - Literary discussion	**Lesson I** 4. Use written language to communicate effectively **Lesson II** 4. Use spoken language to communicate effectively
FEATURING THE FUTURE (SETTING)	**Lesson I:** Travel Brochure - Writing for a specific purpose **Lesson II:** Setting Similes - Creative writing, figurative language	**Lesson I** 4. Use written language to communicate effectively 12. Use written language to accomplish purpose **Lesson II** 6. Use knowledge of figurative language
INTOLERANCE AND INJUSTICE (PLOT)	**Lesson I:** Charting Cause and Effect - Application of sequencing **Lesson II:** Cause and Effect—The Dangerous Diary - Reading for information - Reading for context clues	**Lesson I** 3. Apply comprehension strategies **Lesson II** 3. Interpret text 12. Use spoken and written language to accomplish purpose
JOURNEY: GETTING BACK HOME (PLOT)	**Lesson I:** Literary Locations - Deduction of literary settings **Lesson II:** Analogies—Making the Connection - Word interpretation	**Lesson I** 1. Read wide range of texts (fiction) **Lesson II** 3. Use knowledge of word meaning
MENTOR (CHARACTER)	**Lesson I:** Mentor Acrostic Poems - Writing formula poems **Lesson II:** Limerick Mix Fix - Creative problem solving	**Lesson I** 5. Employment of writing strategies **Lesson II** 12. Use written and visual language to accomplish purpose

ORPHANS (**CHARACTER**)	**Lesson I:** Permission Slip Limericks - Writing formula poems using knowledge of literature **Lesson II:** Orphans in Literature - Application of literary knowledge	**Lesson I** 1. Read wide range of texts (fiction) 5. Employment of writing strategies **Lesson II** 1. Read wide range of texts (fiction)
TO THE RESCUE (**PLOT**)	**Lesson I:** Rescue Round Table - Identifying the answers for specific questions. **Lesson II:** Personification Poems - Writing poems using figurative language	**Lesson I** 11. Participation as a knowledgeable and creative group member **Lesson II** 6. Use knowledge of figurative language
SEA STORIES (**SETTING**)	**Lesson I:** Peter Saves the Day - Dramatic reading **Lesson II:** Sea Stories Selections - Research	**Lesson I** 9. Understanding diverse language use **Lesson II** 12. Use of spoken, written, and visual language to accomplish learning, enjoyment, and exchange of information
STRONG FEMALES (**CHARACTER**)	**Lesson I:** V.I.P. Recipe - Creative writing - Character study **Lesson II:** How Much Do You Know Tic-Tac-Toe - Research	**Lesson I** 5. Employment of appropriate writing strategy **Lesson II** 7. Gather, evaluate, and synthesize data from a variety of sources 12. Use of spoken and written language to accomplish learning, enjoyment, and exchange of information
SURVIVAL IN A HOSTILE ENVIRONMENT (**PLOT**)	**Lesson I:** Survival on Snicket's Island - Creative problem solving - Communication skills **Lesson II:** Zippy Poems - Writing formula poems - Internet research	**Lesson I** 11. Participation as a knowledgeable and creative group member **Lesson II** 8. Use of technology to gather data
TWINS IN LITERATURE (**CHARACTER**)	**Lesson I:** The Twin Times - Newspaper review - Creative wordplay **Lesson II:** Pair Compare - Understanding of word meaning - Knowledge of literary characters	**Lesson I** 1. Read wide range of texts (fiction and nonfiction) 4. Adjust written language to communicate effectively 6. Knowledge of figurative language **Lesson II** 1. Read wide range of texts (fiction) 4. Adjust written language to communicate effectively

CHARACTER CREATION

"No, this is an artificial being, although not, as you believe, a little machine, but a creature of flesh and blood made by human hands. The alchemists of the Middle Ages had great skill in the manufacturing of such creatures. Yes, no doubt about it … this is a genuine homunculus."

—Barnabas Greenbloom, Professor of Archaeology

Featured Fantasy: *Dragon Rider*
by Cornelia Funke

STORY SYNOPSIS

Ancient prophecy is fulfilled when the dragon Firedrake returns to the Rim of Heaven ridden by an orphan boy, Ben; a surly brownie, Sorrel; and the miniature man-made stowaway, Twigleg. Their journey is necessitated by man's encroachment on the dragons' habitat and is made all the more dangerous by the evil Nettlebrand, a human-created dragon slayer. Interesting magical characters populate the tale and human heroes and rodent problem solvers show up just when they are needed.

CONNECTIONS

Could there be any villain as evil as the dragon destroyer, Nettlebrand? What about the wisdom and bravery of the little homunculus, Twigleg? Where did that come from? Both of these interesting and complex characters in Cornelia Funke's *Dragon Rider* were manmade in the laboratory of an ancient alchemist.

Like Shelly's monster of Dr. Frankenstein, sometimes the characters authors create are truly bits and pieces found here and there. Making something from nothing has been a literary theme for a very long time. One only has to read the myths of ancient civilizations to discover the methods of "character creation" are many and imaginative.

RECOMMENDED READING
Fiction

Dr. Jekyll and Mr. Hyde by Robert Lewis Stevenson

Frankenstein by Mary Shelly

Invisible Man by H. G. Wells

Pinocchio by Carlo Collodi

Mythology

D'Aulaires' Book of Greek Myths by Ingri and Edgar D'Aulaire

Illustrated Books of Myths: Tales & Legends of the World by Neil Phillip

Roman Myths by Geraldine McCaughrean

LESSON I: COMPOSITE CHARACTER CREATION

In *Dragon Rider*, Nettlebrand, the massive dragon slayer, and Twigleg, the little homunculus, are out of the ordinary and unforgettable characters. Interestingly, both were magically made in an alchemist's laboratory. This activity allows students to create a unique composite character of their own, using pre-knowledge of literary characters.

Time Required: 35–45 minutes

Objectives

- The students will contribute to a group activity involving the creation of a new and unusual character.

- The students will record information from the group Composite Character Creation Fold Down Data Sheet onto an individual sheet.

- The students may introduce a newly created character to the class.

Materials

- Literary Character List visual (page 12) *(optional)*

- Composite Character Creation Fold Down Data Sheet, one for each student (page 13)

- transparency of Composite Character Creation Fold Down Data Sheet

- Composite Character Creation introduction sheets, one for each student (page 14)

- writing tools

- copies of popular fiction books for student reference *(optional)*

Procedure

1. Prepare the materials ahead of class.

2. Arrange the students in groups of four or five.

3. Introduce the lesson by asking students to think of a favorite literary character. It is a good idea to suggest that they choose a character with a name that begins with the same initial as the student's first or last name; this allows for a variety of characters. (If the students have a difficult time with this task, use the Literary Character List on page 12. Please make the students aware that they are not limited to the characters listed.)

4. Tell the students that they will be asked to write down some information concerning their character. Inform them that they should leave nothing blank. For example, if they do not know a character's age, it is fine to write "very old" or "a kid." If they do not know if the character has a nickname, they may be creative and make one up. Willy Wonka might be called "Candy Man." A good name for Yoda might be "Wise Guy."

5. Display a visual of the data sheet and quickly review what needs to be listed. You may want to use Santa Claus as an example:

   First Name: Santa

   Middle Name or Nickname: Jolly Elf

   Last Name: Claus

   Age: Young at Heart

   Gender: Male

   Place of Residence: The North Pole

   Hair Color: White

   Unique Personality Trait: Gives toys to good children around the world

   Unusual Physical Characteristic: Tummy jiggles like a bowl full of jelly

   Favorite Article of Clothing: Red suit with white fur trim

6. Tell the students that they are to remain true to the character they have chosen while recording the information on each line. Once they have recorded the information, they should fold the paper under so the next person will not know what they wrote.

7. Pass out a data sheet to each student. Tell them that when instructed, they are to pass their papers to the right. If one person in the group gets stuck, then the entire group is stuck because no one may be skipped.

8. Allow five to seven minutes for the students to complete the task. (Be sure to monitor them to keep the process moving.) When the sheets are completed, the student in possession of the sheet unfolds it to reveal a new character.

9. Pass out an introduction sheet for each student to fill out using the data collected.

10. Give the students an opportunity to share the interesting characters with their group members. Allow each group to pick the most unique character to share with the class.

LESSON II: NAME THAT CHARACTER!

Often writers name characters to reveal something about their personality or physical appearance. For example, in *Dragon Rider,* Twigleg had very skinny legs; the mountain dwarf, Gravelbeard, had a gray beard; and Firedrake was a male fire-breathing dragon. This quick and creative activity will get the students' imagination flowing as they conjure up some interesting character names of their own.

Time Required: 20–30 minutes

Objectives

- The students will create names for fictional characters using a basic description.

- The students will share and discuss name choices with the class.

Materials

- Name that Character activity sheet (page 15)

- writing tools

Procedure

1. Prepare the activity sheet prior to the lesson. The activity may be done individually or in groups.

2. Discuss that authors often name characters in their stories to reveal something about that character. Ask for examples of this from the students. (Characters from the Harry Potter series are usually given as examples. Draco meaning "dragon" and Dumbledore meaning "bumblebee" are often volunteered.)

3. Give each student or group a copy of the activity sheet. Allow 10–15 minutes for completion.

4. Discuss the students' responses.

5. Encourage students to create interesting character names of their own and to write a descriptive paragraph describing their new character.

COMPOSITE CHARACTER CREATION

LITERARY CHARACTER LIST

A — **Albus Dumbledore** *(Harry Potter)*

B — **Bilbo Baggins** *(The Hobbit)*

C — **Cruella de Vil** *(101 Dalmatians)*

D — **Dorothy** *(The Wizard of Oz)*

E — **Ebenezer Scrooge** *(A Christmas Carol)*

F — **Frankenstein**

G — **Goldilocks**

H — **Captain Hook** *(Peter Pan)*

I — **Ichabod Crane** *(The Legend of Sleepy Hollow)*

J — **James Henry Trotter** *(James and the Giant Peach)*

K — **Captain James T. Kirk** *(Star Trek)*

L — **Little Red Riding Hood**

M — **Meg Murray** *(A Wrinkle In Time)*

N — **Nearly Headless Nick** *(Ghost—Harry Potter)*

O — **Count Olaf** *(Series of Unfortunate Events)*

P — **Paul Bunyan**

Q — **Quasimodo** *(The Hunchback of Notre Dame)*

R — **Rumpelstiltskin**

S — **Sherlock Holmes**

T — **Tinker Bell** *(Peter Pan)*

U — **Dolores Jane Umbridge** *(Harry Potter and the Order of the Phoenix)*

V — **Violet Baudelaire** *(Series of Unfortunate Events)*

W — **Willy Wonka** *(Charlie and the Chocolate Factory)*

X — **Xena** *(Warrior Princess)*

Y — **Yoda** *(Star Wars)*

Z — **"Zero": Hector Zeroni** *(Holes)*

COMPOSITE CHARACTER CREATION

Fold Down Data Sheet

FIRST NAME:

MIDDLE NAME OR NICKNAME:

LAST NAME:

AGE:

GENDER:

PLACE OF RESIDENCE:

HAIR COLOR:

UNIQUE PERSONALITY TRAIT:

UNUSUAL PHYSICAL CHARACTERISTIC:

FAVORITE ARTICLE OF CLOTHING:

COMPOSITE CHARACTER CREATION

Using the data you collected, fill in the form below.
Be prepared to share this unique character with the class.

Introducing ...

_____ _____ _____ is a _____-

    First Name   Middle Name   Last Name   Age

year-old _____ living in _____. One day, while

         Gender   Place of Residence

scratching the _____ hair on a determined head, _____

          Hair Color   First Name

decided that it was time to have an adventure. It did not matter that others made fun of his/her

_____. After all he/she did have _____.

  Unique Personality Mannerism   Unusual Physical Trait

Therefore, _____ smiled, put on an old _____, and headed

        First Name   Favorite Article of Clothing

out the door to start an interesting tale all his/her own.

Character Sketch

NAME THAT CHARACTER

Writers often pick names for their characters that seem to fit them just right. For example, the school bully might have a "tough name" like Butch Harmon or Slugger Armstrong or Chip Carver. Think of three good names for the characters described. Be prepared to share your names with the class.

Three good names for a small, freckled sixth grader who loves to draw might be:

- ■
- ■
- ■

Three good names for a bizarre, but smart babysitter might be:

- ■
- ■
- ■

Three good names for an elementary school physical education teacher might be:

- ■
- ■
- ■

Three good names for a mysterious new student from Germany might be:

- ■
- ■
- ■

Three good names for a small town's chief of police might be:

- ■
- ■
- ■

EXTRA CREDIT:

Three really bad names for a high school's star football player might be:

- ■
- ■
- ■

ENGLAND: LONG AGO

"I don't want to write about Abner and Ner and Ishbosherth and Joab and Asahel, especially not in Latin. I want to write my own life here in the Marches, between England and Wales. My own thoughts, which keep changing shape like clouds. I am thirteen and I want to write my own fears and joys and sorrows."

—Arthur de Caldicot

Featured Fantasy: *The Seeing Stone*
(Arthur Trilogy Book One)
by Kevin Crossley-Holland

STORY SYNOPSIS

Twelfth-century England is an interesting time to live, but not an easy one. The first book in a trilogy is told in the words of bright 13-year-old Arthur, second son of Sir John Caldicot. This young man's inquisitive nature often gets him in trouble around the castle as he goes about his studies in the classroom and in the courtyard. His life becomes more complicated when Merlin, a mysterious friend of the family, gives him a magical piece of obsidian.

The reader learns about life in the Middle Ages through young Arthur's narrative and about the Arthurian legend through the revelations of the "seeing stone."

CONNECTIONS

With its castles, kings, and crusades, the Medieval era is a setting often used in fantasy literature. The social structure in Tolkien's Middle-earth is very similar to Europe's feudal system. C. S. Lewis's Narnia has many parallels to England's Middle Ages. (Interestingly, the author of *The Seeing Stone* had both of these men as professors when he was a student at Oxford.)

This fascinating time period is also used in popular historical fiction. Examples include

Karen Cushman's *Catherine, Called Birdy* and *The Midwife's Apprentice* and Avi's *Crispin: The Cross of Lead*. The Arthurian legend itself has been the focus of many fine works of young adult fiction. Included in these titles are T. A. Barron's The Lost Years of Merlin series and Jane Yolen's *Sword of the Rightful King: A Novel of King Arthur*.

RECOMMENDED READING

The Canterbury Tales by Geoffrey Chaucer

Ivanhoe by Sir Walter Scott

King Arthur and His Knights of the Round Table by Roger Green

The Once and Future King by T. H. White

The Prince and the Pauper by Mark Twain

Robin Hood of Sherwood Forest by Ann McGovern

LESSON I: ARTHUR'S JOURNAL

More than anything in the world, young Arthur de Caldicot wants to be a squire. To his dismay, his left-handedness makes him awkward at swordsmanship and useless with a lance. He is, however, a true wordsmith. His penmanship is excellent, his vocabulary extensive, and his desire to record his observations and feelings very strong. Keeping a journal is something that would be second nature to Arthur.

Time Required: 30–40 minutes

Objectives

- The students will be introduced to journals and a fictional journal entry.

- The students will create a fictitious journal entry using random prompts of who, where, when, and why.

- The students will demonstrate previous knowledge of certain aspects of the Middle Ages.

Materials

- Arthur's Journal visual (page 19)

- Arthur's Journal activity, one for each student or group (page 20)

- writing tools

- device for selecting topic (Dice work well as there are six choices in each box.)

- a selection of books dealing with the Middle Ages and the Arthurian legend, both fiction and nonfiction, for students to use as reference and/or to check out for their reading pleasure *(optional)*

Procedure

1. Display the visual. Read and discuss it with the class.

2. Explain that this journal entry does not actually exist in *The Seeing Stone*. However, it is based on an event that did happen in the book.

3. Pass out the activity sheets along with the selection device. Students may work individually or in groups.

4. Read the directions on the activity sheet to the students. Allow three minutes for topic selection. (It's a good idea to collect the device after selection!)

5. Encourage students to write with the "voice" of a boy in the Middle Ages.

6. Allow 10–20 minutes for writing.

7. Encourage students to share their entries with the class.

LESSON II: DIARY, JOURNAL, AND LOG

The differences between the types of writing a person uses to chronicle the significant events in his or her life are subtle. Is he keeping a ship's log or a daily journal? Is she writing a diary or her memoirs? Is the distinction even that important? This fun activity will get the students thinking about word connotation and how we use words interchangeably.

Time Required: 20–25 minutes

Objectives

- The students will be introduced to definitions of journal, diary, record, memoir, and log.

- The students will participate in a teacher-directed activity using the Diary, Journal, and Log visual.

Materials

- Diary, Journal, and Log visual (page 21)

- water-soluble pen

- books that are written as diaries or journals to share with students *(optional)*
  For example: *Diary of a Drummer Boy* by Marlene Targ Brill; *Journal of Joshua Loper: A Black Cowboy, The Chisholm Trail, 1871* by Walter Dean Myers; and *Pedro's Journal: A Voyage with Christopher Columbus* by Pam Conrad

Procedure

1. Display the visual. Read the definitions to the class.

2. Ask students if they know of any examples of diaries, journals, or logs.

3. Conduct a classroom discussion using the three listed questions. While answers may vary, certain responses are common.

Examples:

How are the definitions of a diary, journal, and log alike? *They are records and observations. They are written or recorded on a regular schedule. (Note: Students have pointed out that today documentation of one's observations does not need to be written. Video and audiotapes are very good ways to record things for future reference.)*

How are they different? *They have different word histories. One is done only while traveling. (It has been noted that all three are good methods of recording travel events.)*

What are some reasons a person might want to keep a diary, journal, or log? *To help them remember what happened. To keep a record of what happened for future reference. Journals help keep people busy during stressful or sad times. A person may just love to write.*

Why would diaries, journals, and logs be important to historians? *History writers who want to know what happened in the past can read what people living at that time thought. It is good to get the common person's view on life rather than just the kings' and generals' opinions.*

4. Solicit responses for the question asked in the What Do You Think? section of the visual. It does not matter that the students may not know these names from literature or history because there are no right or wrong answers. There are, however, some that work better than others. Students should be able to articulate the reason they chose diary, journal, or log.

Captain Kirk of the Star Ship Enterprise (from Star Trek fame) kept a verbal CAPTAIN'S LOG.

Tom Riddle, a student at Hogwarts School of Witchcraft and Wizardry (from *Harry Potter and the Chamber of Secrets*) created a magical DIARY that allowed him to come back to life.

Captain Meriwether Lewis, eighteenth-century explorer (leader of Thomas Jefferson's Corps of Discovery) did keep a daily JOURNAL on his quest into the nation's interior.

Anne Frank, Jewish girl in hiding during World War II, was a young writer who died in a German concentration camp. The DIARY of Anne Frank has become a classic tale of hardship and survival.

Petra Andalee, sixth grader at the University of Chicago Laboratory School, the young protagonist from Blue Balliett's book *Chasing Vermeer,* keeps what she calls a notebook. It could also be described as either a DIARY or a JOURNAL.

AN OBSERVATION: For some reason the students tend to assign diary writing to females and journal keeping to males.

ARTHUR'S JOURNAL

Arthur de Caldicot tells of his life in the year 1199 AD in *The Seeing Stone* by Kevin Crossley-Holland. Arthur wishes to write his own thoughts and observations rather than copy passages from existing books. If Arthur had kept a daily journal, a written description of day-to-day events, one of his entries might have looked like this.

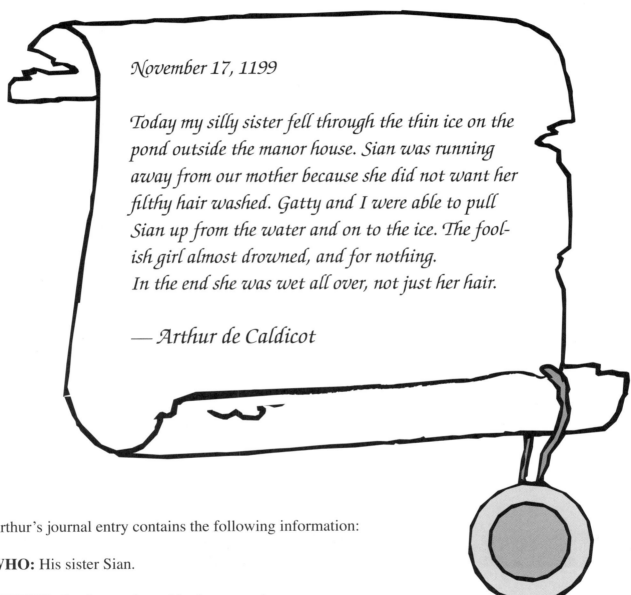

November 17, 1199

Today my silly sister fell through the thin ice on the pond outside the manor house. Sian was running away from our mother because she did not want her filthy hair washed. Gatty and I were able to pull Sian up from the water and on to the ice. The foolish girl almost drowned, and for nothing.
In the end she was wet all over, not just her hair.

— Arthur de Caldicot

Arthur's journal entry contains the following information:

WHO: His sister Sian.

WHERE: On the pond outside the manor house.

WHEN: That day (November 17, 1199).

WHY: To avoid getting her hair washed.

ARTHUR'S JOURNAL

Using a die, spinner, or device of your own choosing, select and circle one item from the Who? Where? When? Why? boxes below. Using these, write a journal entry pretending you are a 13-year-old boy living in the Middle Ages. Be prepared to share your entry with the class.

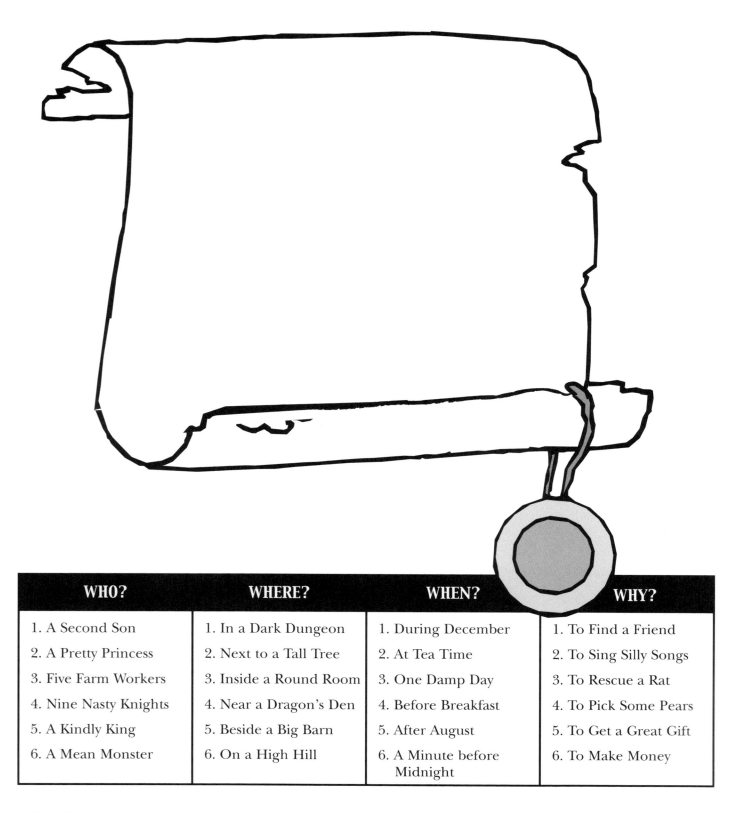

WHO?	WHERE?	WHEN?	WHY?
1. A Second Son	1. In a Dark Dungeon	1. During December	1. To Find a Friend
2. A Pretty Princess	2. Next to a Tall Tree	2. At Tea Time	2. To Sing Silly Songs
3. Five Farm Workers	3. Inside a Round Room	3. One Damp Day	3. To Rescue a Rat
4. Nine Nasty Knights	4. Near a Dragon's Den	4. Before Breakfast	4. To Pick Some Pears
5. A Kindly King	5. Beside a Big Barn	5. After August	5. To Get a Great Gift
6. A Mean Monster	6. On a High Hill	6. A Minute before Midnight	6. To Make Money

Diary, Journal, and Log

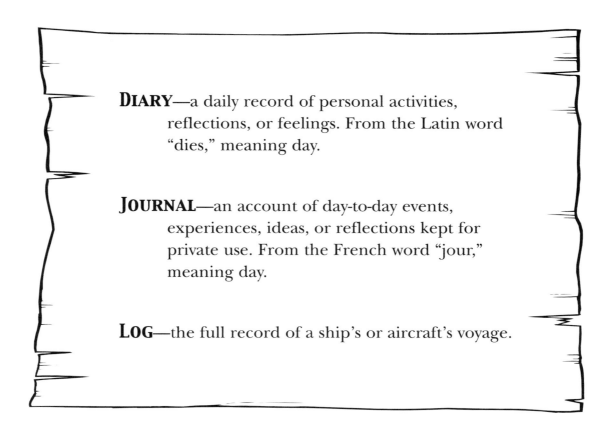

DIARY—a daily record of personal activities, reflections, or feelings. From the Latin word "dies," meaning day.

JOURNAL—an account of day-to-day events, experiences, ideas, or reflections kept for private use. From the French word "jour," meaning day.

LOG—the full record of a ship's or aircraft's voyage.

For Discussion

- How are the definitions of a diary, journal, and log alike? How are they different?
- What are some reasons a person might want to keep a diary, journal, or log?
- Why would diaries, journals, and logs be important to historians?

What Do You Think?

If the following people were to record their daily experiences, do you think they would say they were keeping a diary, journal, or log? Why?

- Captain Kirk of the Star Ship Enterprise
- Tom Riddle, a student at Hogwarts School of Witchcraft and Wizardry
- Captain Meriwether Lewis, eighteenth-century explorer
- Anne Frank, Jewish girl in hiding during World War II
- Petra Andalee, sixth grader at the University of Chicago Laboratory School

Featuring the Future

"They looked out into a cave so enormous that it seemed almost as big as the world outside. Far down at the bottom shone a cluster of lights. 'It's Ember,' Lina whispered."

—Lina discovering the secret of Ember

Featured Fantasy: *The City of Ember*

by Jeanne DuPrau

Story Synopsis

What exactly is going on in the City of Ember? The storehouses are empty, the generator is failing, and even the potato crop is corrupted. It appears no help will be coming from the town's leader, a vile man with only his self interest at heart. It is left up to young Lina Mayfleet and Doon Harrow to try to save the population from a decaying situation. With the help of a cryptic note and much bravery they just might discover the answer to the way out of the strange City of Ember.

Connections

Time travel, predicting the future, and Earth in an alternate universe are several ways authors use to weave interesting and thought-provoking tales. These stories are often cautionary in nature and contain the theme of man's cavalier treatment of humanity and the environment.

Recommended Reading

A Connecticut in King Arthur's Court by Mark Twain

The Ear, the Eye and the Arm by Nancy Farmer

The Giver by Lois Lowry

Time Cat by Lloyd Alexander

Time Machine by H. G. Wells

The War of the Worlds by H. G. Wells

Lesson I: Travel Brochure

A well-written tale includes a setting that can be imaginary but seems very real. This setting may be one that the reader would like to visit. What better way to entice visitors then by creating an interesting and informative travel brochure.

Time Required: 40–45 minutes

Objectives

- The students will exhibit knowledge of a fictional setting by creating a travel brochure.

- The students will follow a specific format for the creation of an informational promotional tool.

Materials

- Travel Brochure visual (page 24)

- Travel Brochure Guidelines visual (page 25)

- paper, pencils, coloring tools

- examples of "real" travel brochures *(optional)*

Procedure

1. Prepare the materials ahead of class.

2. Tell the students that they will be creating a travel brochure and ask if they know the purpose of one. (Possible answers: To advertise, get visitors, attract tourists, and get them to spend money.)

3. Display visual. (A paper copy of the visual may be created and used as an example.) Explain that this is a travel brochure created for EMBER, an imaginary place in a book by Jeanne DuPrau. Read the information on the visual with the students.

4. Display the guidelines visual. (You may also want to have "hard copies" of these guidelines for the students to use in their work areas.) Review the criteria for the activity with the students.

5. Tell the students that they are to pick a setting from a favorite book and create a travel brochure featuring the setting. (Be prepared for the students to select books that are also popular motion pictures.) Encourage students to use copies of their chosen literary works for reference.

6. Pass out materials. Allow 20–30 minutes for completion.

7. Allow students to share their work with the class. Finished brochures make an excellent display.

LESSON II: SETTING SIMILES

When the lights went out in Ember, the author Jeanne DuPrau writes, "Darkness slammed up in front of her like a wall." This is an example of a creative simile. In this lesson students are encouraged to break away from the common clichés and create similes that are unique.

Time Required: 25–30 minutes

Objectives

- The students will define the literary terms simile, cliché, and setting.

- The students will create unique similes.

Materials

- Simile, Cliché, and Setting visual (page 26)

- water-soluble marker

- Setting Similes activity (page 27)

- pencils

- dictionaries and thesauri for student reference *(optional)*

Procedure

1. Prepare the materials ahead of class.

2. Display the visual and review the definitions and examples of simile, cliché, and setting with the students.

3. Solicit students' suggestions for similes for:

   The schoolhouse was like …

   The autumn day was as crisp as …

   The bell sounded like …

   Record at least two student examples for each example on the transparency.

4. Pass out the activity sheets. Allow ten minutes for students to work. (Students may work individually or in groups.)

5. Encourage students to share their similes with the class.

TRAVEL BROCHURE

The City of Ember by Jeanne DuPrau

Motto

"There is no place but Ember. Ember is the only light in the dark world."

—The City of Ember

Directions to the City of Ember

The City of Ember can be found by following an underground river into a very deep and large cavern.

~Visitors Please Note~
Ember is difficult to locate and once located is just as difficult to leave.

Welcome to the City of Ember

The Places of Ember

While in Ember visit the:

- Gathering Hall
- Pipeworks
- Ember School
- Greenhouse
- Supply Depot
- Many Shops

The People of Ember

The population of Ember is:

- Hard-working
- Kind
- Vegetarian
- Civil minded
- Fearful of being without light

The Problems of Ember

While Ember is a wonderful place, please consider the following during your visit:

- There may be a power failure at any time
- Food is limited
- Technology is primitive
- You will not need sunscreen, hats, or umbrellas
- You will need flashlights, matches, and candles

TRAVEL BROCHURE GUIDELINES

Motto	*Directions*	*Welcome*
Use a theme from the story or create your own motto (slogan, saying, or catchphrase) that would be appropriate for the story's setting.	Map/Written Instructions 	Interesting Illustration

The Places	*The People*	*The Problems*
List places of interest and include illustrations. • • • •	• What is the population like? • How many people live in this place? • What do they do for a living?	Is there a problem with this place or is it too good to be true? Remember, your goal in a travel brochure is to make tourists want to visit. Try to make even a horrible situation sound inviting.

 Using a blank sheet of paper and the guidelines above, create a travel brochure about a setting in one of your favorite books.

SIMILE, CLICHÉ, AND SETTING

A SIMILE is a comparison that uses "like" or "as."

- Example: She was falling like the price of Halloween candy on November 1st.

A CLICHÉ is an overused expression.

- Examples: "slow as molasses" and "quick like a bunny"

A SETTING is the time and place of a story.

- Example: In Jeanne DuPrau's book, *The City of Ember*, the location of the story is underground and it takes place sometime in the future.

The City of Ember

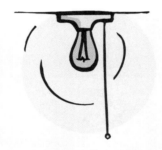

Without using clichés, create similes for the following:

The schoolhouse was like _____

_____

_____.

The autumn day was as crisp as _____

_____

_____.

The bell sounded like _____

_____

_____.

SETTING SIMILES

Choose five of the settings listed and write a unique simile describing it.
Avoid using clichés.

1   A cabin in the mountains
_____
_____

2   A big city in the future
_____
_____

3   The beach after a storm
_____
_____

4   The planet Mars
_____
_____

5   A castle in Scotland
_____
_____

6   The bedroom of teenage twins
_____
_____

7   The front lawn of the White House
_____
_____

8   A town's new candy store on opening day
_____
_____

9   A zoo at midnight
_____
_____

10   Your choice
_____
_____

INTOLERANCE AND INJUSTICE

"'Offend Dobby!' chocked the elf. 'Dobby has never been asked to sit down by a wizard—like an equal—'"

—Dobby, the Malfoy's mistreated house-elf

Featured Fantasy: *Harry Potter and the Chamber of Secrets*

by J. K. Rowling

STORY SYNOPSIS

After his first eventful year at Hogwarts School of Witchcraft and Wizardry, Harry returns to the home of his hateful Uncle Vernon and hard-hearted Aunt Petunia. Here he spends another wretched summer where he is treated with intolerance and loathing. On his birthday, Harry is visited by the ill-treated house elf, Dobby, who gets him in a great deal of trouble. The Weasley brothers rescue Harry when they show up in a flying car and take him away to spend the time before school starts at their wonderful home. Once the term begins, Harry finds his second year as eventful as his first. He must contend with a braggart of a new Defense Against the Dark Arts teacher; the continued cruelty of the bully Draco Malfoy; and the prejudices of his classmates when they discover Harry can speak the language of snakes, parselmouth. Things go from bad to worse when it is revealed that the Heir to Slytherin has returned to open a deadly secret chamber for the sole purpose of destroying all the Mudblood students, those who have a Muggle parent. The story comes to a climax when Harry must fight the mysterious Tom Riddle and a monstrous basilisk to save the life of Ginny Weasley.

CONNECTIONS

The fact that life is not always easy and often unfair is something we would rather our children learn through literature than experience for themselves. (This desire, of course, only happens in a perfect world.) In fact some of the most read books are those where the protagonist must deal with gross intolerance and injustice.

RECOMMENDED READING

Anne Frank: The Diary of a Young Girl by Anne Frank

The Cay by Theodore Taylor

Holes by Louis Sachar

Maniac Magee by Jerry Spinelli

Mississippi Bridge by Mildred D. Taylor

Number the Stars by Lois Lowery

The Outsiders by S. E. Hinton

The Star Fisher by Laurence Yep

To Be a Slave by Julius Lester

View from Saturday by E. L. Koningsburg

The Watsons Go to Birmingham—1963: A Novel by Christopher Paul Curtis

LESSON I: CHARTING CAUSE AND EFFECT

Is there any excuse for intolerance and injustice? Probably not, but there may be some causes for this behavior that lead directly to some undesirable effects.

Time Required: 30–35 minutes

Objectives

- The students will define, understand, and apply the concepts cause and effect.

- The students will complete a chart using specific information.

Materials

- Charting Cause and Effect visual (page 31)

- water-soluble marker

- Charting Cause and Effect activity (page 32)

- writing tools

- books dealing with intolerance and injustice for interested students (*optional*)

Procedure

1. Prepare the materials before class.

2. Explain to the students that things happen due to a chain of events. You may wish to pick a current event, state the incident, and then ask the students what they think might be the causes leading up to it. Tell the students that causes and effects will be the topic of today's lesson.

3. Display the visual. Read the definitions of cause and effect to the students.

4. Complete the chart with the help of the students, writing in the correct answers.

Visual Answers:

CAUSE "Why Did it Happen?"	EFFECT "What Happened?"
The boys broke the rule concerning being out of their room after dark.	The boys were punished and had to spend four hours in detention.

A nasty young man's rich father was able to purchase all new sports equipment for the school's team.	The boy was voted the most popular student in the school and made captain of the team.
The shy girl received a terrible haircut and was teased and made fun of all day.	She went into her room and cried herself to sleep.
Ron was exhausted after staying up all night looking for his lost pet.	He went to bed early without doing any homework.

5. Pass out the activity sheets and writing tools. Read over the directions with the students and check for understanding.

6. Allow students to work individually or in groups.

7. Check as a group.

Activity Answers

CAUSE "Why Did it Happen?"	EFFECT "What Happened?"
The students were astonished when Harry Potter was able to talk to a snake.	Students started saying bad things about Harry, thinking he may be the Heir to Slytherin.
The man often bragged and took credit for others' accomplishments.	He disappointed people when he was unable to do what he said he could do.
Some students misbehaved during fencing club.	All scheduled club meetings were canceled.
The wand was broken and the spell backfired.	The boy was spitting slugs out of his mouth for hours.
Reading was one of the girl's favorite things to do.	She was one of the best students in her class.
The sports team cheated and did not play by the rules.	Points were deducted from the final score and they lost the game.

LESSON II: CAUSE AND EFFECT— THE DANGEROUS DIARY

What causes people to act in a certain way? It may be their personality, others around them, or maybe just an unrelated chain of events. Students will get the opportunity to examine a character's motivation by reading a short passage, answering questions, and discussing their interpretations.

Time Required: 20–30 minutes

Objectives

- The students will review the concepts of cause and effect.

- The students will read for context clues.

- The students will discuss answered questions.

Materials

- Cause and Effect: The Dangerous Diary activity (page 33)

- writing tools

Procedure

1. Prepare the activity sheets before class. Students may work individually or in groups.

2. Explain to the students that this activity deals primarily with the concepts of cause and effect. Explain that the answers they write will be discussed and that they should be prepared to explain them.

3. Read the story to the students if there are struggling readers in the class.

4. Allow about ten minutes for the students and complete the activity sheet.

5. Discuss as a group. Possible answers:

   a. Why was the girl attending a boarding school? *(Her entire family went there. She wanted a good education.)*

   b. Why was the girl lonely? *(Because she was shy. She had no friends.)*

   c. Name two ways the shy girl avoided having to speak to anyone. *(She would sit at the back of the classroom. She would read books during mealtime.)*

   d. What might be the effects of the girl finding that someone has written her a reply in her diary? *(She would be happy to have a friend. She could think someone at school had gotten into her stuff and she would be angry. She might be frightened and destroy the diary.)*

   e. The title of this unfinished story is "The Dangerous Diary." What do you think might happen next to the shy young girl? *(Answers will vary. She could get angry and then hurt someone when she threw the diary at him or her. An evil person might be telling her to do bad things.)*

CHARTING CAUSE AND EFFECT

- A **cause** is WHY something happens. Out of two events, it happens first. To find a cause ask, "Why did it happen?"

- An **effect** is WHAT happens because of a cause. Of two linked events, it is the one that happens second or last. To find an effect ask, "What happened?"

Use the statements below to complete the chart by writing the most appropriate cause or effect in the blank spaces.

CAUSE: "WHY DID IT HAPPEN?"	EFFECT: "WHAT HAPPENED?"
The boys broke the rule concerning being out of their room after dark.	The boys were punished and had to spend four hours in detention.
A nasty young man's rich father was able to purchase all new sports equipment for the school's team.	
	She went into her room and cried herself to sleep.
Ron was exhausted after staying up all night looking for his lost pet.	

Answers:

- He went to bed early without doing any homework.

- The boy was voted the most popular student in the school and made captain of the team.

- The shy girl received a terrible haircut and was teased and made fun of all day.

CHARTING CAUSE AND EFFECT

- A **cause** is WHY something happens. Out of two events, it happens first. To find a cause ask, "Why did it happen?"

- An **effect** is WHAT happens because of a cause. Of two linked events, it is the one that happens second or last. To find an effect ask, "What happened?"

Use the statements below to complete the chart by matching a cause with the most appropriate effect.

CAUSE: "WHY DID IT HAPPEN?"	EFFECT: "WHAT HAPPENED?"
The students were astonished when Harry Potter was able to talk to a snake.	Students started saying bad things about Harry, thinking he may be the Heir to Slytherin.

- The man often bragged and took credit for others' accomplishments.

- All scheduled club meetings were canceled.

- The wand was broken and the spell backfired.

- He disappointed people when he was unable to do what he said he could do.

- She was one of the best students in her class.

- The sports team cheated and did not play by the rules.

- Points were deducted from the final score and they lost the game.

- Some students misbehaved during fencing club.

- The boy was spitting slugs out of his mouth for hours.

- Reading was one of the girl's favorite things to do.

CAUSE AND EFFECT: THE DANGEROUS DIARY

Read the story beginning below. Answer the questions that follow.

- A **cause** is something that happens. Out of two events, it happens first.

- An **effect** is what happens because of a cause. Of two linked events, it is the one that happens second or last.

> **The Dangerous Diary**
>
> *A shy young girl, wishing to get a good education, was away from home for the first time. She had been excited at the thought of attending the same boarding school that all the other members of her family had, but now she found herself homesick and friendless.*
>
> *This young girl was shy and disliked talking to anyone. She even sat in the back of the room in all her classes hoping her teachers would not call on her to answer any questions. Meals were a difficult time for her, too. She would sit by herself and read a book while she ate. Her classmates thought she was a snob and paid no attention to her at all. The only way she had of expressing what she was feeling was through her writing. One of her going-away-to-school presents from her mother had been a diary. Every night before going to bed she wrote down her thoughts and feelings of the day.*
>
> *One night, when she opened her diary to record the events of another lonely day, a surprise awaited her. There, after the entry of the night before, was a written reply. In red ink, in well-formed printed letters, was written, "My Dear Friend, I'm sorry you had a bad day. I think I know something that might make you happy. Would you like me to tell you what it is?"*

1. Why was the girl attending a boarding school? _____

2. Why was the girl lonely? _____

3. Name two ways the shy girl avoided having to speak to anyone.

   a. _____ b. _____

4. What might be the effects of the girl finding that someone had written her a reply in her diary?

   _____

5. The title of this unfinished story is *The Dangerous Diary*. What do you think might happen next to the

   shy young girl? _____

   _____

Journey: Getting Back Home

Today, the road all runners come,
Shoulder-high we bring you home,
And set you at your threshold down,
Townsman of a stiller town.

—poem recited by Mentor, Village's teacher

Featured Fantasy: *Messenger*

by Lois Lowry

Story Synopsis

Lois Lowry brings together several characters from her books *The Giver* and *Gathering Blue* in the interesting, if unsettling, book *Messenger.*

In a fictional, but familiar, society struggling with complex social issues, we find our inquisitive protagonist, young Matty. Matty lives with Seer, a wise blind man, and has the responsibility of being Village messenger. His unique ability to travel through the hostile forest will prove his undoing when he is unable to return home after an ill-fated mission to rescue Seer's daughter.

Connections

The adventures of lost and misplaced characters as they strive to find their way is one of the oldest recorded literary themes. The reader's attention is captured as the struggle is recounted and the quest accomplished. From Homer's *The Odyssey* to L. Frank Baum's *The Wonderful Wizard of Oz*, the goal of our protagonist is always to return to the best place of all—home.

Recommended Reading

Alice in Wonderland & Through the Looking Glass by Lewis Carroll

Gulliver's Travels by Jonathan Swift

The Incredible Journey by Sheila Every Burnford

The Odyssey by Homer

Peter Pan by J. M. Barrie

Pinocchio by Carlo Collodi

The Wonderful Wizard of Oz by L. Frank Baum

Lesson I: Literary Locations

When the plot of a tale includes a character's quest to return home, the location this character has been relocated to is often strange and dangerous. If it were wonderful, would our hero or heroine be so desperate to leave?

Time Required: 25–30 minutes

Objectives

- The students will participate in a competitive literature game.

- The students will review the classical literary works and the uniqueness of various fictional locations.

- The students will discuss the literary themes of journey, quest, and returning home.

Materials

- Do You Know the Literary Location? visual (page 37)

- Literary Location Clues visual (page 38)

- Literary Location Clues Answer Sheet (page 39)

- pencils or pens

- copies of the books noted in the lesson available for students to check out *(optional)*

Procedure

1. Prepare the materials prior to class.

2. Introduce the lesson by asking the students the following questions:

   Why might an imaginary setting make a story interesting? *(Possible answers: Thinking of unusual places is fun. The author is not restricting his characters to places that really exist. Readers like to use their imaginations.)*
   Why might a literary character be in an imaginary setting? *(Possible answers: It's their home. They may be looking for something, saving someone, or be on a quest.)*
   What might be a goal of a literary character on a journey or quest? *(Possible answers: They are going somewhere, looking for something, or returning home.)*
   Why is "home" the place where most characters want to be? *(Possible answers: It is safe. It is where friends and family are. The character may be needed at home.)*

3. Explain that this lesson will test their knowledge of unusual settings in popular stories. Display the visual from page 37. Keep the bottom clues covered. Read the visual with the students. Model the activity by writing down their suggestions. (Hogwarts was used due to the mainstream popularity of the Harry Potter books and movies.)

4. Explain to the students that you will now display and read clues for five settings or "literary locations." They may write one guess on each line after each clue is given. They may change their answer on the next clue, but

they are not allowed to go back and change an answer. When all five clues have been given and the answer is revealed, they may circle the number next to the first time they had written the correct title. This will be the number of points earned for that round of questions. You may choose to give the students credit for the exact location and/or the title of the literary work.

5. Pass out the answer sheets.

6. Display the visual from page 38, revealing one clue at a time. (Discourage any "blurting out" of possible answers by awarding no points for that round to the guilty party.)

7. Evaluate students' knowledge by using the informal scale below.

Evaluation

The students may tabulate their scores by adding the eight numbers that have been circled together and recording on their answer sheet.

Rating:

- 25–20 EXCELLENT—True "Clue Master"

- 19–14 VERY GOOD—Well-Read or "Good Guesser?"

- 13–9 FAIR—Passable paper but nothing to brag about

- 8–0 POOR—"Clueless" concerning literary locations

LESSON II: ANALOGIES—MAKING THE CONNECTION

Most standardized tests include a vocabulary section using analogies. This quick activity is one that works well to get students in test-taking mindset while having a little fun with words and literature.

Time Required: 20–25 minutes

Objectives

- The students will review the structure of an analogy.

- The students will participate in an activity dealing with analogies.

Materials

- Analogies: Making the Connection activity (page 40)

- writing tools

Procedure

1. Decide if you will use the activity as a teacher-directed visual or an individual student worksheet. Prepare the materials.

2. Read the activity introduction to the students.

3. Ask the students to explain the analogy example: Germany is to Europe as United States is to North America. The relationship is Country to Continent.

4. Ask for more examples that would fit this relationship. (Be careful and do not allow the students to substitute states for countries.)

5. Allow the students 5–10 minutes to complete the activity.

6. Check for understanding. Answers: 1. Sky; 2. Puppet; 3. Horn; 4. Return; 5. Queen of Hearts; 6. Write; 7. Eat; 8. Purr; 9. Mischief; 10. Hands.

7. If time allows ask the students to explain the relationship between the items.

DO YOU KNOW THE LITERARY LOCATION?

Hidden below are five clues to an imaginary literary location. Can you guess where it is or in what piece of literature it can be found? Give suggestions after each clue is revealed. The first time the right place or title is written down, we will have earned the number of points listed next to that clue.

5

This place is subject to change.

_____

_____

4

Made of stone, it is cold and damp and surrounded by water.

_____

_____

3

The flora and fauna located near this place can be dangerous.

_____

_____

2

The four houses here compete in yearly contests.

_____

_____

1

Young Wizards and Witches receive their education in this school.

_____

_____

Answer: Hogwarts School for Witchcraft and Wizardry in the Harry Potter series by J. K. Rowling.

LITERARY LOCATION CLUES

#1

5. This city's entrance is watched over by the Guardian of the Gates.

4. It is necessary to wear protective eyeglasses within the city walls.

3. Citizens living here appear to have green skin and wear green clothes.

2. Streets are lined with beautiful houses built of green marble.

1. The home of the throne room of the Great Oz.

Answer: The Emerald City in *The Wonderful Wizard of Oz* by L. Frank Baum.

#2

5. This fictional nation is an island.

4. This island's inhabitants take a shipwrecked doctor prisoner.

3. Mildendo, the main city, is surrounded by a wall two-and-a-half-feet tall.

2. This city is an exact square, each side measuring 500 feet.

1. Here, Gulliver is a giant and referred to as the Man-Mountain.

Answer: Lilliput, a miniature island in *Gulliver's Travels* by Jonathan Swift.

#3

5. This strange place was discovered after a long fall.

4. The food here can change a person's size and shape.

3. A Cheshire Cat in a tree gives directions to lost visitors.

2. Tea parties are held outside the home of the March Hare and the Mad Hatter.

1. The land's monarch, the Queen of Hearts, loves to say, "Off with their heads!"

Answer: Wonderland from *Alice in Wonderland* by Lewis Carroll.

#4

5. A fictional Mediterranean island where lawless giants live.

4. The island is covered with trees and the home of many wild animals.

3. The one-eyed giants on this island live in caves.

2. The lost sailors hiding in the cave escape by hiding under the sheep.

1. The hero, Odysseus, blinds the brutal Cyclops with a timber from a fire.

Answer: Island of Polyphemos, the Cyclops, Book IX of *The Odyssey* by Homer.

#5

5. This constantly changing place is in the ocean.

4. It is said to be a mile long and is dark, wet, and dangerous to be in.

3. Toward the end of this place is a table with a lighted candle on it.

2. Once the home of a ship full of supplies, it now contains only an old man.

1. The old man and his "son," a puppet, escape through the mouth of this place.

Answer: The belly of the shark (whale) in *Pinocchio* by Carlo Collodi.

LITERARY LOCATION CLUES

Answer Sheet

Name: _____

#1

5. _____
4. _____
3. _____
2. _____
1. _____

5. _____
4. _____
3. _____
2. _____
1. _____

#2

#3

5. _____
4. _____
3. _____
2. _____
1. _____

5. _____
4. _____
3. _____
2. _____
1. _____

#4

#5

5. _____
4. _____
3. _____
2. _____
1. _____

ANALOGIES: MAKING THE CONNECTION

Analogies are used to show connections between pairs of words. They usually explain something unfamiliar by comparing it to something well known.

> Analogies are often written in this form:
> a:b::c:d (this is read as, a is to b as c is to d)

Example: Germany is to Europe as United States is to North America

USE THE WORDS IN THE WORD BANK TO COMPLETE EACH ANALOGY.

1. Ship:Ocean :: Hot Air Balloon: _____

2. Peter Pan:Boy :: Pinocchio: _____

3. Cyclops:Eye :: Unicorn: _____

4. Lost:Found :: Leave: _____

5. Neverland:Captain Hook :: Wonderland: _____

6. Book:Read :: Journal: _____

7. Tea:Drink :: Tarts: _____

8. Dogs:Bark :: Cats: _____

9. Lions:Bravery :: Monkeys: _____

10. Shoes:Feet :: Gloves: _____

WORD BANK

Mischief	Return
Puppet	Horn
Sky	Write
Hands	Eat
Queen of Hearts	Purr

MENTOR

"Keep in mind that many people have died for their beliefs: it's really quite common. The real courage is in living and suffering for what you believe in."

—Brom, Eragon's Mentor

Featured Fantasy: *Eragon*

by Christopher Paolini

STORY SYNOPSIS

Written by young Chris Paolini, *Eragon* chronicles the adventures of a poor orphaned farm boy as his unpretentious life is confounded by the discovery of a rare dragon egg. Once the egg hatches and Saphira emerges, it becomes necessary for Eragon to leave his home and search for his destiny. Accompanying the boy and the dragon is Brom, a mysterious storyteller who becomes Eragon's mentor. Their adventures are full of peril as they make their way across a dangerous land searching for their destiny while trying to avoid the notice of the king, a deranged man who thinks only of revenge.

CONNECTIONS

It is a good thing when young troubled protagonists have an older and wiser person to help them out. Not all mentors are wise wizards such as Merlin, Gandalf, and Professor Dumbledore. Wisdom can be found in older siblings, such as Conner Kane's half-sister, Margaret, in E. L. Konigsburg's *Silent to the Bone*. In *Everything on a Waffle,* Miss Bowzer, an eccentric owner of the restaurant, turns out to be a wonderful mentor for Primrose. And in *Because of Winn-Dixie,* Opal's wonderful Gloria Dump could set the standard for the most unconventional mentor of all time.

RECOMMENDED READING

Adventures of Huckleberry Finn by Mark Twain

Because of Winn-Dixie by Kate DiCamillo

Everything on a Waffle by Polly Horvath

The Giver by Lois Lowry

The Hobbit by J. R. R. Tolkien

Ruby Holler by Sharon Creech

Silent to the Bone by E. L. Konigsburg

LESSON I: MENTOR ACROSTIC POEMS

Young people often feel that they are going through life on their own, without help and understanding from the adults around them. During the teaching of this lesson might be a good time to start a dialogue with the students about the mentors in their own world as well as the ones found on the printed page.

Time Required: 25–30 minutes

Objectives

- The students will complete a creative "Acrostic Poem" activity.

- The students will review the concept of synonyms.

Materials

- Marvelous Mentor: An Acrostic Poem (page 44)
- dice or other method for 1–6 number selection
- paper
- writing tools

Procedure

1. Introduce the lesson by displaying the visual.

2. Read the introduction and the definition of an acrostic poem to students.

3. Discuss the directions for the activity at the bottom of the visual. Review the concept of synonyms with the students, explaining that all the words listed are synonyms for the word "mentor."

4. Allow the students to choose one of the six pairs of synonyms listed. (Dice work well.)

5. Explain that the students may choose one of the words of the pair to use for the poem. (If they do both, they may get extra credit.) Students may work individually or in pairs.

6. Pass out paper and pencils and allow students about ten minutes to complete the activity.

7. Encourage students to share their creations with the class.

Lesson II: Limerick Mix Fix

Every well-informed student should be able to identify the rhyme scheme and format of a limerick. This lesson is designed for the students who enjoy working with manipulatives.

Time Required: 20–30 minutes

Objectives

- The students will correctly arrange lines of poetry to create limericks.

- The students will create a title for the limerick.

Materials

- Limerick Mix Fix visual (page 45)
- water-soluble marker
- prepared poetry strips (Limerick Mix Fix Strips from page 46)
- envelopes
- Limerick Mix Fix Recording Sheet (page 47)
- writing tools

Procedure

1. Prepare the materials ahead of class. Calculate the required number of Limerick Mix Fix Strips, prior to class. Photocopy the strips, cut them out, and place them in envelopes. (Because the strips can be used multiple times, it works well if different colors of paper are used for each set. This makes it easier to keep the sets from getting jumbled up.)

2. Display the visual and read it with the students.

3. Using the mixed-up lines, solicit suggestions for the correct order of the limerick. Write the reconstructed poem on the transparency. Possible Solution:

   There once was a man of great size
   Who was good, kindhearted, and wise.
   Though he looked scary,
   He liked Harry
   Being able to symphathize.

4. Create a title for the limerick. (Past examples: "Helpful Hagrid," "A Big Helper," "Scary but Kind.")

5. Pass out envelopes containing the strips, writing tools, and copies of the recording sheet.

6. Inform the students that there are ten lines of poetry in each envelope, enough to recreate two five-line limericks.

7. Read the directions on the recording sheet to the students.

8. Allow 10–15 minutes for the completion of the activity sheet. Suggested solutions:

There once was a wizard Merlin
With white hair on his head and chin.
Magic man, diplomat,
Flowing cloak, pointed hat,
Could Dumbledore be Merlin's twin?

A wizard from Middle-earth old
Was Gandalf the Gray it is told.
His return to the Shire
Made Hobbits inquire,
Would Frodo go looking for gold?

9. Encourage the students to share solutions and titles with the class.

10. Instruct the students to return the strips to the envelopes at the end of the lesson.

MARVELOUS MENTOR

An Acrostic Poem

Young Eragon, the hero in *Eragon* by Christopher Paolini, appreciates the advice he receives from the storyteller, Brom. Brom is Eragon's mentor. Eragon would like to write a poem about his beloved mentor.

An **Acrostic Poem** is a poem in which the beginning letters of a word are written vertically and used to start a word or a phrase that describes that word. The poem below is an example of this type of poem.

> **M** ature
> **E** xpecting the best
> **N** ear in times of need
> **T** eacher, talker, thinker
> **O** bserving the world
> **R** eady to help

Use a selection device to select a number to a word pair. Then choose one of the pairs of listed synonyms for mentor and write a meaningful acrostic poem. Create a title for your poem. You may illustrate it if you wish.

1. Adviser or Coach

2. Counselor or Director

3. Guide or Guardian

4. Helper or Instructor

5. Sage or Supporter

6. Teacher or Tutor

LIMERICK MIX FIX

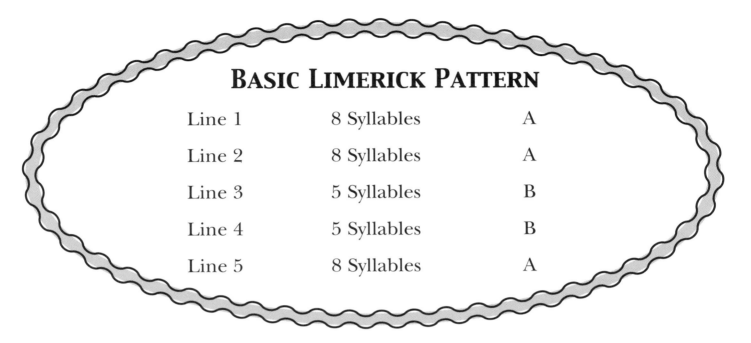

A Limerick is a five-line poem that is usually descriptive and funny. Lines one, two, and five rhyme, as do lines three and four.

BASIC LIMERICK PATTERN

Line 1	8 Syllables	A
Line 2	8 Syllables	A
Line 3	5 Syllables	B
Line 4	5 Syllables	B
Line 5	8 Syllables	A

Can you rearrange the lines below to form a limerick? Once complete, give the poem a title.

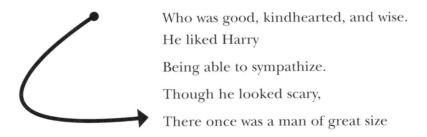

Who was good, kindhearted, and wise.
He liked Harry

Being able to sympathize.

Though he looked scary,

There once was a man of great size

Title: _____

Line 1 _____

Line 2 _____

Line 3 _____

Line 4 _____

Line 5 _____

LIMERICK MIX FIX STRIPS

There once was a wizard Merlin

With white hair on his head and chin.

Magic man, diplomat,

Flowing cloak, pointed hat,

Could Dumbledore be Merlin's twin?

A wizard from Middle-earth old

Was Gandalf the Gray it is told.

His return to the Shire

Made Hobbits inquire,

Would Frodo go looking for gold?

LIMERICK MIX FIX RECORDING SHEET

Use the poetry strips in the envelope to create two limericks. Write your solution on the lines below. Create an interesting title for each poem.

LIMERICK #1

Title: _____

Line 1 _____

Line 2 _____

Line 3 _____

Line 4 _____

Line 5 _____

LIMERICK #2

Title: _____

Line 1 _____

Line 2 _____

Line 3 _____

Line 4 _____

Line 5 _____

ORPHANS

*"In the same boat, you an' me, aren' we Harry? Yeah ... I've said it before ... Both outsiders like ...
An' both orphans. Yeah ... both orphans."*

—Rubeus Hagrid, Hogwarts Gamekeeper

Featured Fantasy: *Harry Potter and the Order of the Phoenix*
by J. K. Rowling

STORY SYNOPSIS

Harry Potter leaves the inhospitable house of his aunt and uncle to spend the rest of the summer with the Weasley family before returning for his fifth year at Hogwarts School of Witchcraft and Wizardry. This will be a dark and dangerous year for all those in the Wizarding World as the malevolent Lord Voldemort has resurfaced with two goals in mind: the return to power and the destruction of Harry.

CONNECTIONS

Young Harry Potter is, without a doubt, one of the most well-known orphans in the world. The fact that Harry has no parents and that the very villain determined to destroy him killed them is one of the major plot lines in the series. Tragically in *Harry Potter and the Order of the Phoenix,* Voldemort kills the closest person Harry has to a parent, Sirius Black, his beloved Godfather.

Stories of adventure and mystery need to have compelling characters that find themselves in complex situations. Young characters without the wisdom of caring adults to guide them are compelling ... and very often get into some interesting and dangerous situations.

RECOMMENDED READING

Adventures of Huckleberry Finn by Mark Twain

Adventures of Tom Sawyer by Mark Twain

Anne of Green Gables by L. M. Montgomery

Crispin: The Cross of Lead by Avi

Dave at Night by Gail Carson Levine

David Copperfield by Charles Dickens

Great Expectations by Charles Dickens

Heidi by Johanna Spyri

The Little Princess by Frances Hodgson Barnett

Milkweed by Jerry Spinelli

Oliver Twist by Charles Dickens

Pollyanna by Eleanor Porter

Secret Garden by Frances Hodgson Burnett

LESSON I: PERMISSION SLIP LIMERICKS

What is Harry Potter going to do? He has no one to sign his permission slip to visit the wizard village, Hogsmeade. In fact, what is any young person without parents supposed to do about permission slips and the like? This lesson introduces a new method of writing a note to the teacher: the Permission Slip Limerick.

Time Required: 25–30 minutes

Objectives

- The students will be introduced to limericks.

- The students will create a limerick using knowledge of various literary works.

Materials

- Permission Slip Limerick visual (page 51)

- Permission Slip Limerick activity (page 52)

- writing tools

- rhyming dictionaries

Procedure

1. Prepare the materials prior to class.

2. Display the visual. Review the information with the class.

3. Create a limerick that includes a student's name and the name of your school using the formula below. (The students will be impressed!)

   (Student Name) a student from (School's Name) School

   Thinks reading good books is real cool.

   Great stories are read

   When going to bed

   (Student Name) has great dreams as a rule.

4. Pass out the activity sheets. Students may work individually or in groups.

5. Allow 10–15 minutes to complete the activity. Have students share their limericks with the class if they wish.

LESSON II: ORPHANS IN LITERATURE

A hero can be defined as someone who overcomes adversity. Being without the guidance of parents is a hardship many strong characters in children's literature must endure. From the classics such as the optimistic *Heidi* by Johanna Spyri and *Pollyanna* by Eleanor Porter, to Charles Dickens's tormented *Oliver Twist* and *David Copperfield,* the poor orphan must find his or her own way in the world.

Time Required: 20–30 minutes

Objectives

- The students will complete an activity sheet.

- The students will discuss the unique situation of an orphan and how it contributes to a fictional character's need to solve a problem alone.

- The students will apply knowledge of literary characters.

Materials

- Orphans in Literature activity (page 53)

- writing tools

- books featuring orphans as characters for students to check out *(optional)*

Procedure

1. Prepare the activity sheet prior to class.

2. Inform the students that the lesson concerns orphans in literature. Ask the class for the definition of an orphan. (Please be sensitive to the fact there may be students in the group who have lost parents.) Ask if they know of any characters in books who are orphans. (The most common responses are Harry Potter and Lemony Snicket's Baudelaire siblings.)

3. Pass out the activity sheet. Students may work individually or in groups. Because of the diversity of the literary works listed, this activity works best when several students are contributing to the answers.

4. Allow 10–15 minutes for the completion of the activity sheet.

5. Check the student work as a group.

   Answers: PART I 1. C, 2. E, 3. F, 4. B, 5. I, 6. H, 7. D, 8. J, 9. G, 10. A.

PART II What is an orphan? *(Someone without a mom and dad. A child whose parents died.)* Why do orphans in books get into some dangerous situations that other young people seem to avoid? *(They don't have parents telling them what to do. Nobody cares what they do. They are all alone.)* How do you think many stories about orphans often end? *(They get adopted. They find a family. They grow up.)*

PART III Possible Titles: *Crispin: The Cross of Lead* by Avi, *James and the Giant Peach* by Roald Dahl, *Maniac Magee* by Jerry Spinelli, *Missing May* by Cynthia Rylant, *Pictures of Hollis Woods* by Patricia Reilly Giff.

PERMISSION SLIP LIMERICK

A Limerick is a five-line poem that is usually funny. Lines one, two, and five rhyme, as do lines three and four.

BASIC LIMERICK PATTERN

Line	Syllables	Rhyme
Line 1	8 Syllables	A
Line 2	8 Syllables	A
Line 3	5 Syllables	B
Line 4	5 Syllables	B
Line 5	8 Syllables	A

A limerick asking permission for Harry Potter to go with his friends to Hogsmeade might look like this:

HARRY JAMES POTTER'S PERMISSION SLIP LIMERICK

Harry, a young orphan at school

Wishes not to break the new rule.

To Hogsmeade he'll go

This poem lets all know

Staying behind would be too cruel.

A limerick explaining why James Trotter may travel in a Giant Peach to New York City might look like this:

JAMES HENRY TROTTER'S PERMISSION SLIP LIMERICK

Rolling downhill in a big peach

James Trotter will be hard to reach

Flat aunts, what a pity!

He may go to the city

New friends wait for him by the beach.

PERMISSION SLIP LIMERICK

Write a permission slip for a literary character who does not have a parent to write it for him or her. It should be written in the form of a limerick. Limericks have five lines and are usually humorous. (See the pattern below.) Your limerick must use the name of the person who would like to go somewhere, or do something special.

BASIC LIMERICK PATTERN		
Line 1	8 Syllables	A
Line 2	8 Syllables	A
Line 3	5 Syllables	B
Line 4	5 Syllables	B
Line 5	8 Syllables	A

Example: JEFFERY "MANIAC" MAGEE PERMISSION SLIP LIMERICK

I don't care what you say or do
Maniac may live at the zoo.
He'll be very kind
Animals will find
As a friend he's always true blue.

WRITE YOUR OWN PERMISSION SLIP LIMERICK!

TITLE _____

Line 1 _____

Line 2 _____

Line 3 _____

Line 4 _____

Line 5 _____

ORPHANS IN LITERATURE

What do Harry Potter, Huckleberry Finn, Peter Pan, and Maniac Magee all have in common? They are all fictional characters struggling to find their way in the world without the guidance and support of their parents.

PART I

Match the character(s) to book.

___ 1. Sophie

___ 2. Tree-ear

___ 3. Violet, Klaus, and Sunny

___ 4. Pip

___ 5. Sara Crew

___ 6. Will Page

___ 7. Dallas and Florida

___ 8. Henry, Jessie, Violet, and Benny

___ 9. Cosmo Hill

___ 10. Prosper and Bo

A. *The Thief Lord* by Cornelia Funke

B. *Great Expectations* by Charles Dickens

C. *BFG* by Roald Dahl

D. *Ruby Holler* by Sharon Creech

E. *A Single Shard* by Linda Sue Park

F. *The Bad Beginning* by Lemony Snicket

G. *Supernaturalist* by Eoin Colfer

H. *Shades of Gray* by Carolyn Reeder

I. *The Little Princess* by Frances Hodgson Burnett

J. *The Boxcar Children* by Gertrude C. Warner

PART II

Short Answer—Be Prepared to Discuss

1. What is an orphan?

2. Why do orphans in books get into some dangerous situations that other young people seem to avoid?

3. How do you think many stories about orphans often end?

PART III

How many other fictional orphans can you list? (*You may use the back of the paper if more space is needed.*)

1.

2.

3.

4.

5.

TO THE RESCUE

"'Princess!' Despereaux shouted. 'Princess, I have come to save you.'"

—Despereaux Tilling, a mouse on a mission

Featured Fantasy: *The Tale of Despereaux: Being a Story of a Mouse, a Princess, Some Soup and a Spool of Thread*
by Kate DiCamillo

STORY SYNOPSIS

Winner of the prestigious Newbery Award, *The Tale of Despereaux* is a tale of an unlikely hero who defies all odds and rescues the princess. Despereaux is a small mouse with large ears. A sensitive soul, he loves music, literature, and a human princess. He is punished for his nonconformity and manages not only to prevail, but also to set an entire kingdom to rights.

CONNECTIONS

"Desperate times call for desperate measures" the saying goes. Reading about someone in distress and the manner in which the rescue is conducted is exciting and educational. What would the reader do in such a situation? How can this danger be averted? Who will have the courage to save the day? Tales of rescue involve the reader. This is a good thing.

RECOMMENDED READING

Charlotte's Web by E. B White

Door in the Wall by Marguerite De Angeli

Johnny Tremain by Ester Forbes

Matchlock Gun by Walter Edmonds

Pinocchio by Carlo Collodi

LESSON I: RESCUE ROUND TABLE

A rescue can be a complicated task. Much information is needed if it is to succeed. The Rescue Round Table activity takes some extra preparation time, but like any good rescue, it is well worth the effort. (Encourage students to create their own Round Table cards in place of writing a standard book report. It is an excellent method to develop higher thinking skills … and the students love to do it!)

Time Required: 20–30 minutes

Objective

*   The students will participate in a prepared question and answer activity focusing on *The Tale of Despereaux* by Kate DiCamillo.

Materials

*   prepared Rescue Round Table cards (page 56—ideally copied on card stock and laminated)

*   photocopy of page 56 for teacher use

*   multiple copies of *The Tale of Despereaux* for interested students to read (*optional*)

Procedure

1. Prepare the Rescue Round Table cards ahead of class. These cards can be photocopied and cut in horizontal strips. Each card should have a question and an answer. For example, the first card should have the question: "Where does *The Tale of Despereaux* take place?" and the answer to another card's question: "A big kettle of soup was on the king's table in the banquet hall." **Note:** Avoid the temptation of putting the correct answer to the question on the same card as this defeats the purpose of the activity. A front and back of each card is created with the adjoining questions and answers.

2. Tell the students that they will be playing a game based on the Newbery Award winning book, *The Tale of Despereaux* by Kate DiCamillo. They do not have to read the book to play the game, but they do need to be good listeners.

3. Pass out the prepared cards to the students.

4. Instruct the student with the card labeled "First Question Asked" to read the card to the class. (Keep a master copy of the card sheet to help with the progression of the game.) The student with the card that states, "The story takes place within the walls of a castle" answers the question, "Where does *The Tale of Despereaux* take place?" Then that student asks the question written on the card. This continues until the student who asked the first question answers the last one.

LESSON II: PERSONIFICATION POEMS

Despereaux is a mouse. Yet he talks to the king, teaches himself to read, and rescues his true love, the princess. When we give human characteristics to objects, ideas, or animals it is referred to as "personification."

Time Required: 20–30 minutes

Objectives

- The students will be introduced to personification.

- The students will participate in a creative poetry writing activity dealing with personification.

- The students will have the opportunity to illustrate a poem.

Materials

- Personification Poems visual (page 57)

- paper and pencils

- colored pencils or markers

Procedure

1. Prepare the visual.

2. Tell the students that today's activity deals with writing personification poems. Define personification as "figurative language that gives human characteristics to objects, ideas, or animals."

3. Explain that some examples of personification are easy to identify, such as the talking rodents in the Redwall Series by Brian Jacques. Other personification is subtler, as when an author writes, "The chair was warm and inviting and begged the weary traveler it sit down."

4. Ask the students to give examples of personification.

5. Display the visual. Read and discuss it with the class.

6. Pass out paper, pencils, and colored pencils/markers.

7. Tell the students they have ten minutes to pick an item and write a couplet about it, giving it human characteristics. Students may illustrate their poems. They should be prepared to share their creations with the class.

RESCUE ROUND TABLE

First Question Asked

Question: Where does *The Tale of Despereaux* take place?

Answer: A big kettle of soup was on the king's table in the banquet hall.

Question: Who is the main character in this story?

Answer: The story takes place within the walls of a castle.

Question: What was the name of the princess who Despereaux falls in love with?

Answer: The main character is Despereaux, a brave little mouse with very big ears.

Question: Why was Despereaux sent to the dungeon?

Answer: Princess Pea is the name of Despereaux's true love.

Question: Who lived in the dungeon?

Answer: Despereaux was sent to the dungeon for sitting at the foot of the king.

Question: How did Roscuro the Rat feel about light?

Answer: Cruel rats lived in the dungeon.

Question: How did the rat's unusual love for light cause a tragedy in the castle?

Answer: Roscuro was an odd rat. He was fascinated by light.

Question: How did the king react to the rat in the soup?

Answer: The rat's love of light caused him to fall into the Queen's soup.

Question: Why was the servant, Miggery Sow, so hard of hearing?

Answer: The king reacted by outlawing the making and eating of soup.

Question: What did Miggery Sow want to be more than anything else?

Answer: Poor Miggery Sow received too many "good clots to her ears" when she was young and could barely hear.

Question: What did Despereaux take with him to rescue the princess?

Answer: Miggery Sow wanted to be a princess more than anything else.

Question: What was on the king's banquet table at the end of the story?

Answer: Despereaux took a spool of thread and a needle with him into the dungeon to rescue Princess Pea.

PERSONIFICATION POEMS

A couplet is a poem with two lines. Write a couplet that meets the following criteria:

- **The first line introduces and describes a nonhuman.** The nonhuman may be an animal or item.

- **The second line gives the subject humanlike characteristics.** The second line is a statement that ties the contrasting words of the first line together. It should rhyme with the first line.

- Give your poem an interesting title.

- Illustrate your poem.

Examples:

BOOK TALK

The dingy gray book sat on the shelf above her.

One day it shouted, "Please don't judge me by my cover!"

TREE ATTIRE

In summer the tree dressed in leaves of green

But it decorated itself in orange for Halloween.

SEA STORIES

"Black Stache had spent his life at sea; he had long believed that he'd faced the worst that the sea could hurl at him, and that he had nothing more to fear. But seeing this thing coming closer toward him now, Black Stache, for just a moment, was afraid."

—the Pirate Captain's reaction to an approaching storm

Featured Fantasy: *Peter and the Starcatchers*
by Dave Barry and Ridley Pearson

STORY SYNOPSIS

The forever-young Peter Pan and the completely evil Captain Hook are archenemies in J. M. Barrie's century-old classic fantasy, *Peter Pan*. Dave Barry and Ridley Pearson delightfully describe just how this relationship evolved in *Peter and the Starcatchers*. The book opens with a small group of orphans from St. Norbert's Home for Wayward Boys boarding the ship the Never Land. While searching for food aboard this ill-run vessel, Peter, their leader, befriends young Molly and soon both become involved with a mysterious treasure chest full of wondrous starstuff. The reader quickly becomes engaged as pirates, talking porpoises, monstrous crocodiles, mermaids, and a secret society known as Starcatchers intertwine in this remarkable prequel.

CONNECTIONS

Unlike Peter Pan, where most of the action takes place in a nursery or on an island, much of *Peter and the Starcatchers* finds itself on or in the water. Sleek pirate ships, clunky cargo ships, small dories, and reliable longboats serve as meaningful settings as Molly Aster, an apprentice starcatcher, and the orphan boy, Peter, struggle to save the magical starstuff, and even their very lives.

Stories set in the sea, or tales where water is a vital part of the plot, have always been popular. (The ancient accounts of Noah's flood and Odysseus's trip home from the Trojan War come to mind.) Students who enjoy *Peter and the Starcatchers* will naturally be curious about J. M. Barrie's *Peter Pan* and want to read it. From there, the connection to other classic tales of adventures on the high seas is a natural one.

RECOMMENDED READING

Captain's Courageous by Rudyard Kipling

Kon-Tiki by Thor Heyerdahl

Moby Dick by Melville Herman

Mutiny on the Bounty by Charles Nordhoff

The Old Man and the Sea by Ernest Hemingway

The Sea-Wolf by Jack London

Treasure Island by Robert Louis Stevenson

20,000 Leagues Under the Sea by Jules Verne

LESSON I: PETER SAVES THE DAY

The characters in *Peter and the Starcatchers* are very active and vocal. If they aren't screaming and running from crocodiles, they are shouting and flying in the air, trying to rescue their friends. Give students an opportunity to be vocal and active, too. This short, but very popular, activity allows the "inner actor" in all the participants to come out as they stomp feet, wave arms, and snarl "Argh-Argh."

Time Required: 15–20 minutes

Objective

- The students will participate in an interactive, teacher narrated, dramatic story, based on *Peter and the Starcatchers*.

Materials

- "Peter Saves the Day" script (page 61)

- copies of various sea stories for students to check out and read *(optional)*

Procedure

1. Prepare the scripts ahead of time.

2. Introduce the students to the story by explaining that this dramatic reading activity is based on *Peter and the Starcatchers*. Explain that for the drama to be successful, the entire class must participate.

3. Assign roles. (In a small group, all may participate; in a large class, half could take the even numbers and the other half the odd numbers.)

4. Read the script aloud, pausing at the bold-print words to allow for student response. If time allows, read the script twice. The first time would be the rehearsal, the second the main event.

5. Encourage students to write their own dramatic plays.

LESSON II: SEA STORIES SELECTIONS

The sea can be a powerful setting for stories with plots dealing with man's struggle with nature. Whet the students' appetite for all things nautical by letting them participate in various activities that address multiple intelligences.

Time Required: 35–45 minutes

Objectives

- The students will be introduced to the concept of the sea as a setting in literature.

- The students will randomly select an activity with a focus on some aspect of the sea.

- The students will participate in activities giving them the opportunity to apply various skills and interests.

- The students will use appropriate materials and reference tools to complete the activities selected.

Materials

- copies of Sea Selection Activity Cube (page 62) (One for each student or group or dice if the Sea Selection Activity List [page 63] is to be used in place of the student-constructed activity cube.)

- scissors, tape and/or glue, paper, pencils, and markers

- copies of news magazines and newspapers for student use

- dictionaries and atlases

- copies of various sea stories for student reference *(optional)*

Procedure

1. Prepare for the lesson by photocopying the Sea Selection Activity Cubes, or creating a visual of the Sea Selection Activity List and collecting materials and reference books for student use.

2. Introduce the lesson by explaining that man's dealings with the oceans, seas, and rivers of the earth make for compelling stories. State that the water can be a powerful setting for stories with plots dealing with man's struggle with nature. Ask for examples of books and movies that feature the sea as an important part of the story. (Students may volunteer such titles as *Pirates of the Caribbean*, *Titanic*, and *The Perfect Storm*.)

3. Divide the students into groups or allow the students to work individually. (This activity also works well as a component of a learning center.)

4. Give each group a Sea Selection Activity Cube sheet, scissors, and glue or tape and have them cut out the pattern and construct the cube. If time is a factor, forgo the construction of the cubes, display the Sea Selection Activity List, and give each group a die.

5. Instruct the students that once the cube is complete, they are to roll it. (If using the Sea Selection Activity List, the number on the die represents the number on the list.) Upon rolling, they are to complete the task that is face up. You may get creative with this cube and either stretch or condense the lesson depending on the ability of the students and the time available for the lesson. Allowing the students to complete three different activities is a good target.

6. Allow the groups to share one of their completed activities with the class.

PETER SAVES THE DAY
A Dramatic Story

1. Pirates *("Argh -Argh")*

2. Island Folk *(Tongue Clicking)*

3. Pirate Ship *(Wave Arms in the Air)*

4. Walk the Plank *(Footsteps)*

5. Peter *("I Can Fly")*

6. Crocodile *("Yum-Yum")*

7. Lost Boys *("Here We Are")*

8. Black Stache *("Grrrrr")*

It was in the days of **pirates, pirate ships,** and daring adventures on the high seas. During this exciting time, young children easily became **lost boys** and magic allowed our hero, **Peter,** to escape **walking the plank** by flying away.

The **pirates** on the **pirate ship,** *Sea Devil*, were searching for **Peter** and his friends the **lost boys. Peter** and a special treasure chest from the **pirate ship** had been washed overboard during the **pirate's** attack on the cargo ship, the Never Land. The **pirates** and their wicked captain, **Black Stache,** wanted very much to get this treasure chest back.

However, there was a terrible storm and the **pirate ship** was destroyed. **Peter,** the **lost boys,** the **pirates,** and **Black Stache** were all washed ashore on a tropical island. Living on this island were primitive **Island Folk** and a very large and nasty **crocodile.**

The **Island Folk** did not like visitors. The **pirates** and **lost boys** were not welcome here. While the **Island Folk** did not make their visitors **walk the plank,** they tried to feed **Peter** and the **lost boys** to the **crocodile.** (The **lost boys** thought it would have been a much better fate if **Black Stache** had made them **walk the plank.**) All was saved when, at the last minute, **Peter** rescued the **lost boys** from the **crocodile,** the **Island Folk,** and the **pirates.**

SEA SELECTION ACTIVITY CUBE

Cut out the pattern.
Fold into a cube.
Use the dotted lined
flaps to secure
the sides.

With the help of an atlas, make a list of the names of 10 seas found throughout the world.

Using a dictionary, define: sea, ocean, nautical, marine, and maritime. Use each in an interesting book title.

Design a poster that serves the purpose of enticing young people to work at sea.

Much is unknown about the earth's oceans. List and illustrate at least five fantastic facts that <u>may</u> be discovered about it in the future.

What is happening in the water? Find a current event in a magazine or newspaper dealing with some scientific aspect of oceans, seas, lakes, or rivers. Share with class.

Write and illustrate a poem titled either *"I See the Sea"* or *"The Life Of a Sailor."*

SEA SELECTION ACTIVITY LIST

1. With the help of an atlas, make a list of the names of 10 seas found throughout the world.

2. Using a dictionary, define: sea, ocean, nautical, marine, and maritime. Use each in an interesting book title.

3. Design a poster that serves the purpose of enticing young people to work at sea.

4. Much is unknown about the earth's oceans. List and illustrate at least five fantastic facts that <u>may</u> be discovered about it in the future.

5. What is happening in the water? Find a current event in a magazine or newspaper dealing with some aspect of oceans, seas, lakes, or rivers. Be prepared to share it with the class.

6. Write and illustrate a poem titled either "I See the Sea" or "The Life of a Sailor."

STRONG FEMALES

"… As soon as her mother had left for bingo, Matilda would toddle down to the library. The walk took only ten minutes and this allowed her two glorious hours sitting quietly by herself in a cozy corner devouring one book after another. When she had read every single children's book in the place, she started wandering round in search of something else."

—a description of four-year-old Matilda's reading habits

Featured Fantasy: *Matilda*

by Roald Dahl

STORY SYNOPSIS

Young Matilda Wormwood's self-centered and not very bright parents have no idea she is a child prodigy. When they enroll her in Crunchem Hall Primary School, Matilda encounters the appropriately named headmistress, Miss Trunchbull, and the sweet teacher, Miss Honey. Both of these women are strong, but in different ways. The headmistress is physically powerful. This strength does not matter when Matilda applies amazing mental powers to rid the school of her. Once Miss Trunchbull leaves, Miss Honey's financial security is returned. This young woman then shows strength as she takes over the responsibility of raising the now happy Matilda.

CONNECTIONS

Matilda may be a little girl, but she is very much the protagonist in Roald Dahl's tale of the good, small, and smart triumphing over the mean, large, and stupid. Dahl's characters are usually over-the-top and this tale is no exception. What is unique is that while most of the main characters are females, this is a book boys really enjoy reading. Boys are usually quite hesitant to pick up a book that has a title with a female's name in it. Therefore, when suggesting a book with strong female characters, *Island of the Blue Dolphins* and *Out of the Dust* are often the most readily accepted.

RECOMMENDED READING

Anne Frank: The Diary of a Young Girl by Anne Frank

Anne of Green Gables by L. M. Montgomery

Catherine, Called Birdy by Karen Cushman

Island of the Blue Dolphins by Scott O'Dell

Jane Eyre by Charlotte Bronte

Out of the Dust by Karen Hesse

Pride and Prejudice by Jane Austen

Roll of Thunder, Hear My Cry by Mildred Taylor

LESSON I: V.I.P. RECIPE

V.I.P. is an acronym for Very Important Person. A character in a book is a V.I.P. How does an author "cook up" interesting characters? Students will have an opportunity to create their own unique recipes.

Time Required: 25–30 minutes

Objectives

- The students will write a character analysis in a unique manner.

- The students will apply knowledge of literary characters.

Materials

- V.I.P. Recipe visual (page 67)

- V.I.P. Recipe activity (page 68)

- paper and writing tools

- cookbooks for student reference *(optional)*

Procedure

1. Prepare materials ahead of class. **Note:** The activity sheet may be used as a visual, in which case students would record their work on separate pieces of paper.

2. Display the visual. Read the introductions and recipes with the class. Ask the students what these recipes might reveal about the two characters in Roald Dahl's book *Matilda*. *(Possible responses: Miss Trunchbull is sour, nasty, and dangerous. Miss Honey is lovable and generous.)*

3. Tell the students that they will be creating their own recipes for female literary characters. Explain that a recipe contains the instructions for making something, usually food. Recipes list ingredients required, tools needed, and processing directions. Give students permission to have fun. The recipe they create does not have to actually be cooked and eaten!

4. Pass out copies of the activity sheet and review the directions with the class. Students may write their recipes on the back or may use a separate piece of paper. If available, cookbooks may be used for reference to various recipes.

5. Allow 10–15 minutes for students to work. Students may share their recipes with the class. (The students' work can be collected and bound into a class recipe book.)

LESSON II: HOW MUCH DO YOU KNOW TIC-TAC-TOE

Famous females, fictional and historic, were required to make choices in their lives. Students are permitted to make their own choices as to which activities to complete; some include researching others' creativity.

Time Required: 25–35 minutes

Objectives

- The students will select and complete three activities from a grid focusing on famous females.

- The student will use appropriate reference tools for research.

Materials

- How Much Do You Know Tic-Tac-Toe visual (page 69)

- paper and pencils

- reference tools (examples: dictionaries, encyclopedias, card catalogs, and book lists)

Procedure

1. Prepare materials prior to class. (The visual also works well as an individual activity sheet or as a component of a learning center.)

2. Display the visual. Read the directions and review the information on the grid with the class.

3. Ask if there are any questions. Encourage students to be creative with their solutions to the activities. Accept an answer as long as they validate it. (Queen Latifa and Dairy Queen are perfectly good answers for box number seven.)

4. Pass out writing tools and paper.

5. Allow students 15–20 minutes to complete the activity.

6. Check as a group. (See the sample answers on the following page.) Allow students to share their answers with the class.

Sample Answers:

1

Answers will vary (and probably be silly)

2

Sample Couplets

Matilda was small but real bright.
She liked to read all day and night.

Sweet and nice was Miss Honey.
It was sad she had no money.

3

Joan of Arc
Fighting for Freedom

Annie Oakley
Super Sharp Shooter

Amelia Earhart
Flying into Danger

4

Some Fictional Redheads

Pippi Longstocking
Anne of Green Gables
Little Orphan Annie
Caddie Woodlawn
Ginny Weasley
India Opal Buloni *(Because of Winn-Dixie)*

5

Some "Girl Name" Titles

Alice in Wonderland
Amazing Grace
Boston Jane
Catherine, Called Birdie
Eloise
Esperanza Rising
The Great Gilly Hopkins
Madeline

6

Some Fairy Tale Characters

Cinderella
Beauty and the Beast
Goldilocks
Little Red Riding Hood
Little Mermaid
Rapunzel
Sleeping Beauty
Snow White

7

Favorite Queens

Queen Elizabeth II
Queen Victoria
Mary Queen of Scots
Queen Latifa
Queen of Hearts
Queen Nefertiti
Queen Isabella
Dairy Queen

8

Sample Sentence

Carolyn Keene writes Nancy Drew mysteries very well.

9

In the United States, the First Lady, usually the wife of the president, plays the role of hostess. Martha Washington, Abigail Adams, Dolly Madison, Mary Lincoln, Edith Wilson, Eleanor Roosevelt, Jacqueline Kennedy, Nancy Reagan, Barbara Bush, Hillary Clinton, Laura Bush.

V.I.P. Recipe

What if a Very Important Person had a favorite recipe that described her personality perfectly? In *Matilda* by Roald Dahl, Miss Trunchbull is mean and hateful. Her recipe for Agatha Trunchbull's Sour Dough Rolls reflects this. Miss Honey, on the other hand, is sweet and very giving. Can you tell by her recipe for Miss Honey Pie?

Agatha Trunchbull's Sour Dough Rolls

Sift together:

2 cups cactus flour

1 cup salt

1 Tablespoon arsenic

Mix:

1 gallon vinegar

1½ cups sour milk

2 pounds lard

6 rotten eggs

Directions:

Form into oddly shaped balls. Bake at low heat for 6 hours. Serve with a spread made of broken glass shards, sharp tacks, and rusty nails.

Miss Honey Pie

Ingredients:

3 cups white sugar

3 cups brown sugar

1 large bottle of corn syrup

1 can molasses

1 bag miniature marshmallows

2 large jars of honey

Directions:

Mix all the ingredients in a large bowl and let it stand on the counter overnight. In the morning pour into a large chocolate pie crust. Sprinkle with coconut. Serves a class of 24 students.

V.I.P. RECIPE

Choose two female characters from a story you have read. (Need some ideas? You may use any pair in the box below.) Create recipes that reveal something about the character's personality, appearance, and/or profession.

Recipes should also meet the following criteria:

- The character's name in the recipe's title.

- At least six ingredients.

- Cooking instructions.

- Serving suggestions.

Recipes may be illustrated.

Alice & the Queen of Hearts
Alice in Wonderland by Lewis Carroll

Cinderella & Cruel Stepmother
Cinderella (Fairy Tale)

Molly Weasley & Dolores Jane Umbridge
Harry Potter and the Order of the Phoenix
by J. K. Rowling

Dorothy & the Wicked Witch of the West
The Wizard of Oz by L. Frank Baum

Violet Baudelaire & Esme Squalor
A Series of Unfortunate Events by Lemony Snicket

Hermione Hash (Example)

Ingredients:

8 bookworms

12 cat hairs

9 mushrooms

1 cup diced gilly weed

2 gallons of good luck juice

a pinch of sorcerer's sauce

2 tablespoons of wolfsbane

Directions:

Mix together in a black cauldron. Simmer over low heat for 13 hours. Stir occasionally with magic wand. Serve with cold pumpkin juice.

HOW MUCH DO YOU KNOW
TIC-TAC-TOE

This grid contains nine different activities concerning famous females. Choose three activities in any connecting squares across, down, or diagonally. Do your work on a separate sheet of paper and include the number of each activity. Be prepared to share your results with the class.

1 The girl's name Wendy did not exist until J. M. Barrie created it for a character in *Peter Pan*. Create an original name for a girl.	**2** Write a couplet (two-lined, rhyming poem) about a favorite literary female character.	**3** Joan of Arc, Annie Oakley, and Amelia Earhart could be the subjects in three different books. Create titles for these books without using any proper nouns.
4 Red is the color of strength and bravery. List four fictional females with red hair.	**5** List the titles of five books that include a girl's name.	**6** Who are six female characters that appear in either a folktale or a fairy tale?
7 A female monarch is given the title of queen. List seven of your favorite queens.	**8** Write an eight-word sentence describing one of these authors: A. K. Applegate, S. E. Hinton, J. K. Rowling, Carolyn Keene, Betsy Byers.	**9** Define the term "First Lady." List nine First Ladies.

SURVIVAL IN A HOSTILE ENVIRONMENT

"… she was certainly the best inventor who had ever found herself trapped in the gray waters of the Stricken Stream, clinging desperately to a toboggan as she was carried away from the Valley of the Four Drafts, and if I were you I would prefer to focus on the boring phenomenon of water evaporation, which refers to the process of water turning into vapor and eventually forming clouds, rather than think about the turmoil that awaited her at the bottom the Mortmain Mountains."

—the author explaining Violet's dire circumstances

Featured Fantasy: *The Grim Grotto*

by Lemony Snicket

STORY SYNOPSIS

Will the poor Baudelaire orphans find a respite from their unsettled life of misery in this eleventh book in A Series of Unfortunate Events? It appears not. The reader is introduced to some interesting new characters. Captain Widdershins and his stepdaughter, Fiona, rescue the orphans when they invite them to become crewmembers aboard a dilapidated submarine, the Queequeg. There are also characters who the reader might remember from past adventures, such as the optimist Phil and the tap-dancing-ballerina-fairy-princess-veterinarian, Carmelita Spats, who calls everyone she does not like a "cakesniffer." The siblings remain in danger as they fight off attacks by deadly mushrooms, a hook-handed man, and the ever-present Count Olaf.

CONNECTIONS

When the setting of a story is in an environment that is perilous, the reader can be assured that survival will become a major theme. In *The Grim Grotto* the three Baudelaires have to con-tend with an environment so hostile and toxic it almost takes the life of baby Sunny. (As usual, their impressive research skills save the day.) Our students, most of whom live very safe lives, enjoy reading stories about resourceful and brave people who use their wits to survive the elements.

RECOMMENDED READING

Call It Courage by Armstrong Sperry

From the Mixed up Files of Mrs. Basil E. Frankweiler by E. L. Konigsburg

Hatchet by Gary Paulsen

Island of the Blue Dolphins by Scott O'Dell

Julie of the Wolves by Jean Craighead George

My Side of the Mountain by Jean Craighead George

Robinson Crusoe by Daniel Defoe

Swiss Family Robinson by Johann Wyss

The Tempest by William Shakespeare

Lesson I: Survival on Snicket's Island

Combine the popularity of Lemony Snicket's A Series of Unfortunate Events books and television's survivor reality programs and you have a lesson that has the students participating in a creative problem-solving activity that is intellectually stimulating and creative.

Time Required: 35–45 minutes

Objective

• The students will participate in a creative problem-solving group activity.

Materials

• Survival on Snicket's Island visual (page 72)

• Survival on Snicket's Island activity (page 73)

• paper, colored pencils, markers, and rulers

• reference materials, atlases, almanacs, encyclopedias, etc. *(optional)*

Procedure

1. Prepare the materials ahead of class.

2. Divide the class into groups with four or less students in each group.

3. Display and discuss the visual with the students. (You may wish to explain that the author, Lemony Snicket, is a very creative writer, who often gives unique names to the characters and places in his books.)

4. Pass out an activity sheet to each group. Have drawing materials available for student use in a central location.

5. Encourage the students to use reference materials in the naming of the landforms.

6. Allocate 20–25 minutes of activity, then have the student groups present their solutions.

7. Score solutions using the point system on the bottom of the activity sheets.

Lesson II: Zippy Poems

Violet, Klaus, and Sunny Baudelaire often find themselves in some interesting places. In *The Grim Grotto, Book the Eleventh* in A Series of Unfortunate Events, they are rescued from the Stricken Stream, progress to the Gorgonian Grotto, and end up on Briny Beach. All interesting sounding places that might make good titles for poems.

Time Required: 25–30 minutes

Objectives

• The students will create a poem using a specific formula.

• The students will determine the number of syllables in words.

• The students will have the opportunity to research information on the Internet.

Materials

• Zippy Poems visual (page 74)

• Zippy Poems activity (page 75)

• writing tools

• computers with Internet access *(optional)*

Procedure

1. Prepare the visual and activity sheets prior to class. **Note:** This lesson works well as an enrichment activity in a history or geography unit. If specific zip codes are required, prepare a list of the places with their zip codes before class. The Web sites zip4.usps.com/zip4/citytown_zip.jsp and www.50states.com/zipcodes/ work well.

2. Display the visual. Read and review it with the students.

3. Pass out the activity sheets. Students may use local zip codes they know, the ones listed on the visual, or the Internet to look up the zip codes of specific places. It is your call.

4. Allow 10–15 minutes for students to complete the activity. They may share their poems with the class.

SURVIVAL ON SNICKET'S ISLAND

Let's pretend you are about to have the adventure of a lifetime. Lemony Snicket, the author of A Series of Unfortunate Events, has presented a challenge to the young people across the land and you and your team have been selected as contestants. The grand prize is full college tuition for each member of the team that builds the best shelter, gives the most interesting names to various geographic landforms, and writes the best rescue message. (Lemony Snicket is a very strange man.) The island is 10 miles wide and three miles long. It does not have electricity. The temperature is pleasant, cool at night and warm in the day. Fresh water can be found in the crater lake of an inactive volcano. Birds, turtles, insects, and abundant tropical vegetation are native to the island.

TASKS:

- List the members of your team and give your team a name that describes the members in it.

- Create a list of ten items you think will be useful to you on the island. They must fit in a backpack. Each person on the team may have his or her own backpack.

- Give creative names to the following landforms: volcano, lake, beach, cliff, valley, and cave.

- Write a creative rescue message that could be put in a bottle and thrown in the ocean.

- Make a sketch of what your shelter might look like.

- Be prepared to present your solution to the challenge with the class.

SNICKET'S SCORE SHEET

1–10 points	Creative Team Name	_____
1–20 points	Appropriate Items Packed	_____
1–15 points	Landform Names	_____
1–20 points	Rescue Message	_____
1–15 points	Shelter Design	_____
1–20 points	Group Presentation	_____
	Total Points	_____

SURVIVAL ON SNICKET'S ISLAND

Team Members: _____

Team Name: _____

SUPPLY SELECTION

Backpack #1	Backpack #2	Backpack #3	Backpack #4
1.	1.	1.	1.
2.	2.	2.	2.
3.	3.	3.	3.
4.	4.	4.	4.
5.	5.	5.	5.
6.	6.	6.	6.
7.	7.	7.	7.
8.	8.	8.	8.
9.	9.	9.	9.
10.	10.	10.	10.

LANDFORM NAME CHOICES

Volcano _____   Valley _____

Lake _____   Cave _____

Beach _____   Cliff _____

RESCUE NOTE

SHELTER SKETCH

Make a sketch of what your shelter might
look like. List materials used under the sketch.
Use the back of the worksheet.

SNICKET'S SCORE SHEET

1–10 points	Creative Team Name	_____
1–20 points	Appropriate Items Packed	_____
1–15 points	Landform Names	_____
1–20 points	Rescue Message	_____
1–15 points	Shelter Design	_____
1–20 points	Group Presentation	_____
	Total Points	_____

FROM SNICKET TO SHAKESPEARE Survival in a Hostile Environment

ZIPPY POEMS

The zip code used on a letter or package is the routing code used by the United States Postal Service. ZIP is an acronym for the Zone Improvement Plan. The word "zip" also implies that the mail travels more quickly when a zip code is used. The basic zip code consists of five numbers.

The author Lemony Snicket titles many of his books with descriptive place names, such as *The Miserable Mill, The Hostile Hospital, The Slippery Slope,* and *The Grim Grotto.* Some cities and towns in the United States also have names that are very descriptive. Can you think of a name of such a place?

Directions for writing a ZIPPY POEM:

Discover the zip code of an interesting place and write it down vertically. Think of some words and phrases that might describe that place. Write your poem so that the syllables in each line match the number. (**Note:** Zeros count as 10.) Be sure to include the location's name in the poem. Remember to add a title.

Example:

OLD NEW ORLEANS

7   New Orleans is an old place

0   Mardi Gras, Ghosts, French Quarter, Cajun Food

1   Old

2   Spooky

2   River.

Examples of descriptive places with zip codes include:

Beecher Falls, Vermont 05902

Golden Valley, North Dakota 58541

Montpelier Station, Virginia 22957

Orange Grove, Texas 78372

Sea Ranch Lakes, Florida 33308

Stony River, Alaska 99557

Sunspot, New Mexico 88349

Volcano, Hawaii 96785

ZIPPY POEMS

A zip code used on a letter or package is the routing code used by the United States Postal Service. ZIP is an acronym for the Zone Improvement Plan. The word "zip" also implies that the mail travels more quickly when a zip code is used. The basic zip code consists of five numbers.

Can you think of a place with an interesting, descriptive name? Do you know its zip code? (You can research it at the Web site zip4.usps.com/zip4/citytown_zip.jsp.) Write the zip code of your choice down vertically. Think of some words and phrases that might describe that place. Write your poem so that the syllables in each line match the number. [**Note**: Zeros count as 10.] Be sure to include the location's name in the poem. Remember to add a title.

ZIPPY POEM

TITLE: _____

TWINS IN LITERATURE

*"'Twins are when'—he had started to give a scientific explanation, stopped himself—
'when a mother has a litter of two babies instead of one.'"*

—Dennys Murray speaking to Japheth

Featured Fantasy: *Many Waters*

by Madeleine L'Engle

STORY SYNOPSIS

The 15-year-old identical twins Sandy and Dennys Murray are the main characters in this sequel to Madeleine L'Engle's *Swiftly Tilting Planet.* Overlooking a warning note from their mother explaining that a scientific experiment is in progress, they are accidentally sent back to the Biblical period of Noah and the time before the great flood. Here in a harsh desert, they encounter unicorns; tiny wholly mammoths; and good and bad angels, the Seraphim and Nephilim. Using the themes of survival in a hostile environment, and a quest to return home, the author writes another fantastic metaphysical tale.

CONNECTIONS

Twins, from Greek Mythology's Apollo and Artemis to contemporary masters of marketing Mary-Kate and Ashley Olsen, have always fascinated us. It may be the rarity of a multiple birth or the idea of someone having a mirror image, but when twins are the main characters, one can assume that their "twin-ness" will be a major factor in the storyline.

RECOMMENDED READING

Jacob Have I Loved by Katherine Paterson

The Man in the Iron Mask by Alexandre Demas

Ruby Holler by Sharon Creech

Singularity by William Sleator

Twelfth Night by William Shakespeare

LESSON I: THE TWIN TIMES

Newspapers are a fundamental form of communication. While the immediacy of instant information using telecommunications and the Internet has its advantages, the print newspaper still has an important place in our fast-paced society. Clark Kent's Daily Planet and Harry Potter's Daily Prophet are good examples of how newspapers have been used to progress a storyline. This lesson serves as a creative review of the components of a typical newspaper as well as an introduction to the use of twins as main characters in literature.

Time Required: 35–45 minutes

Objectives

- The students will discuss the purposes of local, state, national, and electronic newspapers.

- The students will be introduced to various pieces of literature containing twins as characters.

- The students will complete an activity.

Materials

- The Twin Times visual (page 79)

- The Twin Times activity (page 80)

- writing tools

- copies of newspapers—local, state, and national if possible

- copies of listed literature books, as well as others that may have twins as characters *(optional)*

Procedure

1. Introduce the lesson by explaining to the students that today's activity is twofold. They will be discussing twins in literature and reviewing and doing an activity with the parts of a newspaper.

2. Display examples of various types of newspapers. A good collection would include local, state, and national publications. (A school newsletter and a supermarket "tabloid" are fun additions to the collection.)

3. Discuss with the students the focus and functions of the newspapers available. Point out that each paper has similar features such as news stories, feature stories, editorials, sports reports, information of community interest, and advertising. Point to the headlines and explain how they serve as guides for the subject of the article.

4. Inform the students of the newspapers available in the school's library.

5. Display the visual. Read and discuss it with the students.

6. Pass out the activity sheet. Review the directions and clarify any questions. (You may wish to get the students started by brainstorming some newspaper name ideas. Examples: Romulus and Remus could have a newspaper called Roman Report or the Italian Tattler. Tweedledee and Tweedledum may inspire such names as Looking Glass Letter and Mad Hatter Chatter.)

7. Assure the students that there are no right or wrong responses and encourage them to play with the words they choose. Point out that newspapers often include catchy titles with stories to catch the readers' attention.

8. Allow students 15–20 minutes to work with the activity sheet. Allow students to share their favorite title ideas with the class.

9. Display some of the students' work on a bulletin board titled "Read All About It."

LESSON II: PAIR COMPARE

This lesson can be as simple as a review of how to compare two unrelated objects as complex as an in-depth literary character analysis. It is your choice! Just as twins often have names that rhyme or start with the same letter, the word pairs selected also have similarities. It will be interesting to see if the students observe the alliterative wordplay.

Time Required: 25–40 minutes

Objectives

- The students will make comparisons between two non-related things and/or literary characters.

- The students will complete the activity, Pair Compare and/or Pair Compare Character Challenge, individually or as a member of a group.

- The students will share and discuss answers with the class.

Materials

- Pair Compare and/or Pair Compare Character Challenge activity sheets (pages 81–82)

- writing tools

- a book and a newspaper to use in a demonstration

- books available for student reference: *The Adventures of Pinocchio, Charlie and the Chocolate Factory, Charlotte's Web, The House at Pooh Corner, James and the Giant Peach, The Magic School Bus, Peter Pan, Harry Potter and the Sorcerer's Stone, The Wonderful Wizard of Oz, A Wrinkle in Time*

Procedure

1. Decide which of the two activity sheets is more appropriate to use with your class. (If both are used, the lesson will take about 40 minutes.) The activity sheets may also be made into transparencies and completed as a teacher-directed activity.

2. Introduce the lesson by explaining that it is easy to compare things, such as twins, when they are alike but more challenging to compare things that do not look or act alike.

3. Hold up a book and a newspaper and ask the students to volunteer answers as to what the two have in common. Possible answers: they are both made of paper, include information, and have words and pictures.

4. Tell the students that today's lesson deals with how things are alike and that another word for this is "comparison." Ask what the word is for how things are different. When "contrast" is given, tell the students that they will not be working with contrasts today, only comparisons.

5. Pass out or display the activity sheet of your choice. Allow students to work individually or in groups. (The Pair Compare Character Challenge activity works better when completed as a group activity.)

6. Check as a group. Answers will vary. Praise students for unique thoughtful responses.

Examples of student responses:

Sticks and Stones: Found in nature, used to build, used to hurt people, both have six letters.

James Henry Trotter & Harry James Potter: Both are fictional characters, they have similar names, they have mean aunts, they are orphans, they are English, etc.

The Twin Times

 The Twin Times is an imaginary newspaper that focuses on two-of-a-kind things. Listed are the titles of some of the stories and features included in a typical issue.

Headline Story: Twin Peaks to Host Bicycle Rally

National News: Fuel Prices Double as Twin Tankers Sink off the Coast

Local Feature Story: Annual Twin Convention Held at Poppins Park

Editorial: The Pros and Cons of Dressing Alike

Letter to the Editor: The "Evil Twin" Story Line Overused on Television

Want Ads: Twins Wanted for Doublemint Gum Commercials

Weather: Two Tornadoes Spotted Yesterday—Fair Weather Tomorrow

Entertainment Section

- **At the Movies:** The Clones Come Back

- **In the Bookstores:** *Double the Trouble* by Nary Twice

- **Just out on CD:** Dueling Duets

Sports Section: The Minnesota Twins Are in the Playoffs!

Financial Page: Double Your Investments in Just Two Years

Horoscope: Gemini—"Working with a partner will be twice as profitable."

Comics: Dot and Ditto On Their Own

Advice Column: Abby and Ann's Advice for Anxious Adolescents

Recipe of the Day: Double Fudge Cake

Advertisements: Two-for-One Sale at the Mirror Image

THE TWIN TIMES

Using one of the pairs of twins featured below, create titles for newspaper articles that would reflect the imaginary "world" they live in. Be prepared to share your ideas with the class.

- Romulus and Remus—Roman Mythology

- Tweedledee and Tweedledum—Lewis Carroll's *Through the Looking Glass*

- Phil and Lil DeVille—Rugrats Cartoon

- Fred and George Wesley—Harry Potter series

- Your own choice

NEWSPAPER'S NAME _____

Headline Story: _____

National News: _____

Local Feature Story: _____

Editorial: _____

Letter to the Editor: _____

Want Ads: _____

Weather: _____

Entertainment Section: At the Movies: _____

                                     In the Bookstores: _____

                                     Just out on CD: _____

Sports Section: _____

Financial Page: _____

Horoscope: _____

Comics: _____

Advice Column: _____

Recipe of the Day: _____

Advertisements: _____

PAIR COMPARE

Even if they are different in appearance, twins often have many similarities. The word pairs below have more in common than beginning with the same letter. List three things each twosome has in common. Try to make your answers as unique as you can.

STICK AND STONE

1 _____
2 _____
3 _____

DOG AND DONKEY

1 _____
2 _____
3 _____

SOUP AND SANDWICH

1 _____
2 _____
3 _____

BUCKET AND BASKET

1 _____
2 _____
3 _____

SHIRT AND SLACKS

1 _____
2 _____
3 _____

MOUNTAIN AND MOLEHILL

1 _____
2 _____
3 _____

ROAD AND RIVER

1 _____
2 _____
3 _____

PAIR COMPARE CHARACTER CHALLENGE

CHALLENGE: These literary character pairs may not be twins, but they have many things in common. Choose three of the pairs and list three ways each of the characters are alike. Try to make your answers reflect knowledge of the characters.

James Henry Trotter	Harry James Potter
James and the Giant Peach	*Harry Potter and the Sorcerer's Stone*

1 _____
2 _____
3 _____

Peter Pan	Pinocchio
Peter Pan	*The Adventures of Pinocchio*

1 _____
2 _____
3 _____

Willy Wonka	The Wizard of Oz
Charlie and the Chocolate Factory	*The Wonderful Wizard of Oz*

1 _____
2 _____
3 _____

Meg Murray	Ms. Frizzle
A Wrinkle in Time	*The Magic School Bus Series*

1 _____
2 _____
3 _____

Wilbur the Pig	Winnie-the-Pooh
Charlotte's Web	*The House at Pooh Corner*

1 _____
2 _____
3 _____

FEATURED FANTASY BOOK LIST

Barry, Dave, and Ridley Pearson. *Peter and the Starcatchers.* Hyperion, 2004.

Crossley-Holland, Kevin. *The Seeing Stone.* Scholastic, 2000.

Dahl, Roald. *Matilda.* Viking, 1988.

DiCamillo, Kate. *The Tale of Despereaux.* Candlewick Press, 2003.

DuPrau, Jeanne. *The City of Ember.* Random House, 2003.

Funke, Cornelia. *Dragon Rider.* (Translated by Anthea Bell.) Scholastic, 2004.

L'Engle, Madeleine. *Many Waters.* Atheneum, 1986.

Lowry, Lois. *Messenger.* Houghton Mifflin, 2004.

Paolini, Christopher. *Eragon.* Knopf, 2002.

Rowling, J. K. *Harry Potter and the Chamber of Secrets.* Scholastic, 1999.

Rowling, J. K. *Harry Potter and the Order of the Phoenix.* Scholastic, 2003.

Snicket, Lemony. *The Grim Grotto.* HarperCollins, 2004.